Boris Johnson is a *Daily Telegraph* columnist, and is frequently to be seen on television and heard on radio. He is the Editor of the *Spectator*, and is the Member of Parliament for Henley-on-Thames.

FRIENDS, VOTERS, COUNTRYMEN

Jottings on the Stump

BORIS JOHNSON

HarperCollins*Publishers*

HarperCollins*Publishers*
77–85 Fulham Palace Road,
Hammersmith, London W6 8JB

www.fireandwater.com

This paperback edition 2002
1 3 5 7 9 8 6 4 2

The author thanks John Murray Publishers for permission
to quote from 'Henley Regatta' by John Betjeman

A catalogue record for this book
is available from the British Library

ISBN 978-0-00-711914-1

For Marina

μέγα βιβλίον
μέγα κακόν

Callimachus

Preface

There were no TV cameras to record my last, undignified exit from the political stage. It was 1 May 1997, or rather the early morning of 2 May. The place was the Plas Madoc sports centre in Clwyd South, and events had evolved, in the words of the Emperor Hirohito, not entirely to my advantage. For six weeks we had flogged up and down the streets of old mining villages. I had stood in the drizzle on street corners, ranting in slogans about health, jobs, crime, prosperity.

No one took any notice, except the people who finally flung up their sash windows and told us to hop it. For eighteen months, with the assistance of some tapes, I had learnt the Welsh language, to the point where I could order a pint of beer or fish and chips (*pysgod a sglodion*) and tell a tacsi driver to make for the town centre. As for the Welsh national anthem, which once embarrassed John Redwood, I had it off pat. It was all in vain. I fought Clwyd South, as we candidates put it – and Clwyd South fought back.

As I stood on the platform in the sports centre and heard the returning officer clear his throat, I knew I was about to be thrashed out of sight. Martyn Jones, a bow-tied former biochemist in the brewing industry, was returned with a crushing majority. And it was pretty obvious to me, as the results came in from across the country, that I was less crushed than others. That was the night that Portillo managed to lose a 15,545 majority in Enfield Southgate. It was the worst defeat for 160 years. It was the Tory party's Cannae.

After he had relegated me to a footnote in electoral history, the returning officer turned and asked if I would like to say a few words. Yes, I said, I jolly well would.

Marina afterwards said it was the most graceless speech she had ever heard from a defeated candidate. But my troops, who were looking fairly bedraggled, loved it. Lloyd Kenyon, a Tory bigwig and later expelled from the Lords by Blair, said it was the best he'd ever heard – by me, that is. I think I invoked General MacArthur, who promised he would return from his defeat in the Philippines, and Winston Churchill, and perhaps even Admiral Yamamoto on the subject of Pearl Harbor. The gist of it was that the Tories would recover. 'We will be back,' I promised.

We would fight, fight and fight again. Blair had wakened a sleeping giant, I warned, and in five years' time he would feel our wrath. I knew then that I would try to find another seat, because it looked as though they were ready to rub along without me in Clwyd South, and once the virus is in your bloodstream, there is no getting rid of it.

This is an account of the next election, and my attempt, in another rural seat, to vindicate my promise of revenge. The idea for the book, and indeed the title, I owe to Susan Watt of HarperCollins. But it is an entirely (if not excessively) personal book. It is not a manifesto. It makes no pretensions to being a work of political economy.

WEEK ONE

Nothing for It: The Campaign Begins

Saved by Toast

Friday 11 May

That's it. The gun is fired. We're off. With a glint in his eye Stuart Reid, deputy editor, seizes the reins at the *Spectator*. My *Telegraph* column is prorogued. Chris Scott has drawn up a compendious battle plan, beginning with a walkabout in Henley high street.

Walkabouts generally provoke psychic stress. You can't just walk up and down, beaming. People will try to ignore you. It is necessary to accost them whether they seem interested or not, with the iron nerves of Bruce Anderson at a cocktail party. You also need what Chris calls 'razzmatazz', something to attract attention from a distance, get tongues wagging, children pointing, that kind of thing. This means balloons.

So we all spend ages blowing up a cloud of blue balloons, bearing the words VOTE CONSERVATIVE, and stuff them into the people carrier.

In fact, as we discover when we arrive in the car park of the Argyll pub, we have overdone it. We have about forty blue balloons, all attached to the same knotted skein. There follows a long passage in the pub car park as we try to think of a way of separating these balloons, like grapes, into smaller bunches. None of us has a knife, not even our campaign driver number one, an ex-military man. Step forward James Triptree, a beaming giant. He produces his cigarette lighter, to burn through the Gordian knot. Brilliant, we all say.

The resulting explosions sound like the gunfight at the OK Corral. Daniel Hannan, planet-brain MEP, goes almost purple with laughter, and writhes around, slapping his waistcoat. He cannot believe the aptness with which my campaign has begun. Chris puts the string back in the car, where it starts a small fire in the campaign literature.

Trailing the remnants of this massacre, we arrive at our first stop: the Cancer Relief jumble sale in Henley town hall. You never saw such stuff, a real Aladdin's cave. Only a place like Henley could produce jumble of this quality: rack upon rack of clothes, cashmere skirts and what have you, and some sensational bargains to be had – like the collection of sheets I pick up for the house in Swyncombe, for only £5.

As I never tire of saying, there is such a thing as society, and it's not just the DSS and Meals on Wheels.

It's all the thousands of people in South Oxfordshire who give up their Saturday morning, gratis, to sell sheets or a potted begonia or a double amputee Action Man.

We arrive back at the car to find the campaign literature still burning briskly on the back seat. Chris seizes the sheets, and uses them to smother the blaze.

Feeling we're going well, we head off for lunch with Paul Goodman, who is an old *Telegraph* chum and standing to be the MP in the adjacent seat of High Wycombe. We sit in the garden of a pub in Hambleden, and agree how very pretty it all looks: the Cross of St George on the church, the little white water lilies on the purling stream, the blue sky.

'It's going well,' says Dan Hannan, known to his friends as Wang Dan in honour of the Chinese dissident. 'It's been a good couple of days,' says Dan, who is spending most of his time speech-writing with William Hague on the leader's battlebus.

'Yeah,' say Goodman and I, like a couple of lieutenants admiring Napoleon's battle plan on the eve of Borodino, or possibly Waterloo. 'It's going well for us, this tax thing,' we say. There are Tory posters everywhere, saying YOU PAID THE TAX – WHERE ARE THE TEACHERS, POLICE, NURSES ETC.?

The trouble is, though, I add, with a faint, sheep-like cough, that we still don't seem to be getting through to the people who might have been so obviously Conservative twenty years ago. I mean the people, with children, in their thirties and forties. They hear our point about tax, and they broadly agree with it. But they are also feeling quite well off, and they want good state schools, and they are a bit nervous about this business of paying for health insurance ...

Yeah, we all say, gloomily. Still. There is a useful picture of Cherie on the front page of the paper, kissing some kid in the street. It is, in theory, a good pic for Labour, cheering and, though I blush to say so, rather sexy in an odd sort of way.

But we Tory candidates can see the silver lining. Cherie was meant to have a fourteen-day case, and she wasn't going to do any campaigning. What the picture in fact shows is that Labour has been forced to deploy her prematurely, because they have been so rattled by the pace and aggression of the Tory start.

I suppose the reader is entitled to a better explanation of what I am doing here. Perhaps I'll save up the stuff about my ideals, hopes, ambitions and theory of political representation. Let me just say that it has been quite a long march merely to get to this juncture. The toughest bit, no question, has been the final round of the Henley Tory party selection procedure.

It is anyone's guess quite how I flopped over the finishing line ahead of the rest. Some have said I was doomed to succeed, that too many of the audience were *Telegraph* readers who had come – in spite of what they had read – prejudiced in my favour. Others say it was the schmaltzy joke about toast in maternity wards of the NHS. Me, I think the result was also partly due to the attempts of my enemies to dish me.

You may not have been to Benson – a lovely place, famous for its aerodrome – so you may not know that it has a newish brick village hall which can hold a very big audience. Hmmm, I thought, when we pulled up, and we saw the bonnet-to-bonnet array of shiny Jags and Mercs and – I don't want you to get the wrong idea about the Tory party – plenty of less distinguished marques.

'How many would you say are here?' I croaked to Chris the agent, who was on the door.

'About five hundred,' he said.

I'll tell you why there were so many. It's because this was the first time in a quarter of a century that the South Oxfordshire Conservatives had been asked to make a decision on the identity of their parliamentary candidate. They were there because they cared about the result; because whatever you may think about Tory activists and party members, they are public-spirited people, and they wanted the worthiest successor to

Hezza they could find; and after 214 candidates had bitten the dust, there were three remaining. There was David Platt, a highly intelligent barrister; there was Gill Andrews, a highly intelligent solicitor; and there was me.

We were asked to wait in a sort of seminar room as the crowd flowed in next door, a various bunch – men in hacking jackets, big men in those canary-yellow cords you see in Jermyn Street windows; there were many rather beautiful and distinguished-looking women, some of them pearly, some not; there were posh-looking people, and people who didn't look remotely posh (but who, of course, might have been). At one point I sort of loitered by the door and watched them come in, and noted how some of them beamed at me, and some of them avoided my eye in what I took to be a marked manner, until I was ushered back into the waiting room.

Here we all turned down the offer of a glass of wine (except, I think, for Marina); and we had one of those conversations that if you are lucky you have only two or three times in your life – the sort of tense insincerities a pair of gladiators might deal in before being shoved out into the arena.

It was obvious that David and Gill were good at policy. They had thought about local issues; they had clearly done our hosts the courtesy of mugging up, and I started to feel outclassed. They had been through the system, they were veterans with the scars of many selection procedures upon them, while I was a pansy, an amateur. This was only my second such encounter since I was selected to fight Clwyd South. I had an inkling of the issues: police numbers and Watlington hospital and the cost of housing; but what if they asked me something out of left field, designed to expose my lack of real local knowledge?

Feebly, as one does in these situations, I tried to psych out the opposition. 'Aha,' I said to my colleagues in the green room, 'but what about the climate change levy? What is our policy there?'

They knew all about the climate change levy, as well they might, since it is one of Gordon Brown's less defensible stealth taxes, and it is certainly no false modesty on my part if I say that they were both better than me on that night. I doubt whether Gill or David would dissent.

It was my go first, and the audience, frankly, was not responsive. My friend Nicholas Soames had given me a piece of advice, bawled at me down a mobile phone, as though to some idiotic junior officer lost on manoeuvres. 'Whatever you do, don't give them any jokes,' he said. 'They don't want jokes. They want to know why you might be a good man to represent them.'

So I kept the joke quotient low, and after they had listened in silence for a while I started to wonder why it was so infernally hot in here. Was it the number of people? Or was I in a – help – flop sweat? Someone had said that it was a good idea to extol the beauty of the constituency and, in advance, I had tried a line on Marina about the rolling Chiltern hills, etc. – some piece of Edward Thomas-type lyricism. She said she thought it was pretty cringe-making. So too, when I came to declaim it, did the audience, and it may be that one or two people even rolled their eyes. I staggered to a halt. There was applause, but it would be an exaggeration to say that it made the rafters shake, and then there were questions.

There was schools, and hospitals, and there was Europe. And Europe, and Europe, and Europe. At one point Howard Green, the chairman (a monument of impartiality), had to beg for questions on another subject. I just plugged my line, which I believe to be reasonable, moderate and intellectually unbeatable. You don't want to hear this now, do you? You do? You don't mind?

It goes as follows. Of course we are part of Europe. That is an irrevocable geographical fact. The only way we could cease to be part of Europe would be to tow the British Isles a thousand miles to the west and sink them in the Atlantic. And what is more, I go on to say, we are honoured, paid-up and fully participating members of the European Union. No one could conceivably expel us, nor would it be in the interests of our partners to do so. As for our own interests, they are still on balance served by maintaining our membership. This has brought palpable benefits to Britain in free trade and in bestowing on British citizens the rights of free movement and free establishment in the EU; and withdrawal would mean a potentially worrying loss of influence. But there is a difference between reluctantly accepting the hard necessity of a minimal membership, and submitting to the final goal of the Euro-federalists.

That is why, for instance, I am opposed to more majority voting in the Council of Ministers. This procedure is deeply anti-democratic. Because it means that a cabinet minister, explicitly enjoined by his colleagues to take a certain position, can fly out to Brussels and find himself overruled. What is the point of the great edifice of parliamentary democracy, where voters choose MPs, and MPs form governments, and governments have cabinets, when the whole thing can be squished round the table in Brussels?

For roughly similar reasons I am opposed to British membership of the euro – or scrapping the pound, as we Tories call it. The root objection is that you are taking away the ability of the people to punish those in authority for errors of economic policy (both monetary and fiscal) because you are handing the power to make those decisions to people in Brussels and Frankfurt. I feel I have an advantage in the European question, which is that I spent five years as a reporter in Brussels, sinking from a position of moderate idealism to one of fairly vinegarish scepticism. I know what I am talking about and I know I am right.

And all this, as far as could be told, was going down OK, when someone stood up; and I can see him now in my mind's eye: suited, white-faced. He didn't look particularly friendly. 'Mr Johnson,' he began, with a lot of ictus on the word 'Mister'.

Uh-oh, I thought to myself, this doesn't sound like fun.

'Mr Johnson,' he said again, 'you have lied! You have lied to us in saying that you have no skeletons in your cupboard!'

Like a gigantic vacuum cleaner the audience drew an intake of breath. This sounded bad, some of them were thinking – or perhaps, depending on their point of view, they were thinking that this sounded good.

It is a terrible fact of human existence that we all have a guilty conscience about something. But as it happens I really, honestly, truly don't think I have any skeletons to speak of in my cupboard: moth-eaten clothes, ties from Polish airlines, but no skeletons. So I waited for him to hit me with it and it was the usual thing. It was Guppygate.

You don't know about Guppygate, and you don't care?

Good. Let's leave it at that. It is a tale told by an idiot, signifying nothing, and anyway, if you really want it all, I could perhaps relegate it to a Martin Amis-style appendix or footnote. But the point was that this chap felt he had me skewered, and for one terrible millisecond it seemed he might be right.

What he forgot was the volatility of the audience and their sense of fair play. His question was so long, and so venomous, and so full of recondite detail about a decade-old non-scandal, that by the end of it I guess some people were rather hoping I'd be able to bat the ball back.

'OK,' I said, for the first time feeling rather cool and in control. 'I'm very grateful that you asked that question' (politicians always say this when they are playing for time). 'But in so far as you accuse me of keeping this Guppy business a secret, well, that seems a bit thin, since I have actually been questioned about it on a TV game show watched by I don't know how many millions. I don't think you could get much more public than that.'

Those may not be the exact words, but they are correct in the Thucydidean sense, in that they reflect the meaning of what I said.

They liked it. At any rate, they seemed to feel that this was an adequate answer, and it may be that this – recovering under fire – was important. Which was a bit of bad luck on the other two, since they lacked the advantage of an embarrassing past to brush aside.

Or it may have been that the clincher was after the break, when we all three had to appear together in a *Question Time* type format. I was so convinced that the Guppygate question had sunk me that we had gone to the pub for a beer, and I was in a slightly better frame of mind. Asked about funding of the NHS, I told a positively glutinous story about toast in the maternity wards.

This homily concerns what happens if you accidentally eat your wife's toast in the middle of the night, when she has just given birth, and your wife wakes up and says, I say, what happened to that toast? And you say, I'm afraid it's no longer with us, or not directly with us ha ha ha; and your wife says, Well, what's the point of you? Why don't you go out and hunt stroke gather some more toast, as your forefathers did back in the olden days? And you go into the highways and byways of the maternity hospital, and I tell you, Mr Chairman, there are babies popping out all over the place; and then you find the person who is i/c toast, and you ask for some more, and there isn't any more, of course, Mr Chairman, because you have had your ration, and when you move to open your wallet, you find that this is no good, either. You can't pay for things on the NHS. It's a universal service free at the point of delivery, delivery being the operative word, Mr Chairman, ha ha ha. And the whole point of the saga is that it ought to be possible for a well-heeled journalist, who has been so improvident as to eat his wife's toast in the middle of the night, to pay for some more ... And this is not as trivial as it sounds, because we need to think about new ways of getting private money into the NHS.

If you look at the countries that do better on cancer survival rates, and on coronary heart disease – countries such as Belgium, Germany or France – they do not rely on a monopoly state provider. They have a variety of systems – employer-based insurance schemes, employee-based insurance schemes, whatever; and they manage to spend more per capita on health, and to achieve better results, because they do not just rely on general taxation and spending – the first being electorally unpopular and the second being inefficient.

And if you want an example of the kind of thing on which we could start to spend our own money, without infringing the principle of universality – then I give you toast!

In any case, it's all our own money, one way or

another: it's just that the customer is able to target resources at exactly what he or she wants, viz toast.

Poor David was so nauseated by the whole thing that he was gagging next door to me and rolling his eyes; and some people who have been so unfortunate as to hear the parable of the toast more than once have come up to me and begged me to strike it from the repertoire. But it made a good point, I think, and if it achieved one sneaky psychological trick, it was to put the selectors in mind of Marina, who was sitting in the front row.

And that was it, more or less. We waited in the seminar room and the great throng began to vote, by a secret ballot, with a steady and inscrutable murmur. We took it in turns to declare that the other was the surefire winner (Oh I'm sure you've got it, Boris; No you did it, Gill; Well done, David, etc.), and waited. The first count did not yield a conclusive result. In other words, none of us had achieved 50 per cent support. Gill had the fewest votes, which illustrates, I am afraid, the sexism of the Tory party. She was far better than me but she's a chick, and the trouble with Tory associations is that they don't groove to chicks – a problem I will address later.

So it was between me and Platt for the second ballot. I snuck outside the room to have a look at them again. People had begun to drift away because it was getting late, off to their dinner parties, their baby-sitters. Nothing much happened, and it was drawing later and later. It must have been getting on for 10 p.m. I was pretty sure I was sunk, and was reading the *Henley Standard*, studying the property pages from a position of entirely academic detachment. Then a cheer went up. We all eyed each other. Whose supporters would be so indecorous as to cheer?

The door opened, and the Tory selection procedure continued its ancient and ceremonial pattern. The area agent entered, the representative from Central Office who is there to see fair play. He marched straight up to me, and I assumed I was a goner, because the last time I'd been in this position, the area agent for Wales had gone up to the chap I beat and shaken his hand, and said, hard luck, but he was going to be the bridesmaid again.

But no, he didn't give me the bridesmaid stuff. He congratulated me.

Later we saw ourselves on TV. I appeared to be in a sort of delirium. I felt utterly elated, as though my lungs were full of helium, and vaguely insane.

Being selected is one thing, however. If you want to reach Parliament. That means a year of milling around and shaking hands. And in the last four weeks, it means knocking on doors, hundreds and hundreds of them. Some people say this is pointless, since you can't hope to meet all your 60,000 potential electors. I disagree.

It is striking how seriuosly they take this procedure, the voters in our supposedly apathetic democracy. When they open the door, they know they are taking part in an important transaction. It's an invitation to take a position on national politics, and to judge by their reactions people still feel that is different from an encounter with a double-glazing man or a Jehovah's witness.

For once, in atiny, fractional way, they are in control. They are being asked for their verdict on all that babble they see on the news. They have something you want. They are almost always pleased that you have bothered to solicit it in person. But they feel entitled to be wooed, and to be rude.

Trouble with Women

Saturday 12 May

You get used to canvassing after a while. Your nerves toughen up. Soon you find yourself rather enjoying it, your features contorting themselves reflexively into a Jeffrey Archer leer as you dart at the shoppers.

'I wonder whether I could introduce myself,' I say metronomically outside Waitrose. 'I'm standing to be your local MP.' Sometimes the punters come over all tense and inward, and swivel their trolleys away without meeting your eyes. But a lot of them break into smiles. 'I know exactly who you are,' they may say, 'and I am delighted to see you out here showing your face, and you can certainly count on my support.' You have no idea what joy this response produces in the candidate. More disappointing is: 'Ah yes, well, I am pleased to meet you, but I am sorry to say I shan't be voting for you, because … etc.' One man takes a look at my leaflet, and exclaims: 'Common sense! You had eighteen years to get some common sense!' Scrumple, scrumple.

'That's a good place to stand,' snarls a chap with a pram, pushing past in what I take to be an unsupportive manner. I say it again: it's the yuppies with kids – those are the votes we need; they are the engine of the economy and of politics.

My feeling, having pumped dozens of hands, and stared deep into many many eyes, is that with a month to go we have the support of slightly under half the electorate. Michael Heseltine held 46 per cent of the vote in 1997 …

Our next stop is Thame, a lovely market town, slightly larger than Henley itself, where we launch our programme of action by – you guessed it – having lunch. During my last campaign, in Clwyd South, I had the habit at every campaign lunch of drinking a lot of beer, accompanied by very thick-cut cheese and raw onion sandwiches. This had all sorts of ill-effects. Now David Barrington, the proprietor of the Spread Eagle, produces some more sophisticated stuff, and we stick to Diet Coke.

There must be half a dozen of us having lunch there, but let me introduce first my agent, Chris Scott. In so far as my campaign shows any signs of professionalism it is thanks to Chris. He knows where I am going, what I am doing, and shows an uncanny instinct for political trouble. For instance, he is very keen that I should avoid doing debates on Europe, since I am apt to become Euro-sceptical, and some of the association are less sceptical.

Chris is a highly intelligent, saturnine fellow in his late twenties, who is clearly destined to run the Tory party machine – at least if the Tories have any sense. He takes a mischievous pleasure in my pessimism. He addresses me formally, though without any real reverence, as 'Candidate'.

As we canvass the shopping precinct afterwards, Diana Ludlow, our county council candidate, grabs my arm and whispers. 'Here,' she says, pointing up at a café on the first floor. 'They've been watching you from the window. You should go up and say hello.'

'Oh – do you really think so?' I say, feeling none too keen to go up and glad-hand some people who are probably quite happy having lunch.

'Go on,' says Diana. 'They'll expect it,' she says. 'They'll feel offended if you don't.'

'Are you sure?' I ask her.

'Positive,' she nods.

With a heavy heart I mount the stairs, to find a young couple at work behind a counter, making toasted sandwiches.

'Hello, good afternoon. I'm so sorry to trouble

you, but I wonder if I could introduce myself. I'm standing to be your ...'

'We're from Aylesbury,' says the man, meaning not from this constituency. 'Now bloody well go away.'

How can you put up with it? people ask me. Why are you doing it? they keep saying. Sometimes they sound admiring, sometimes suspicious. The honest answer, though perhaps not a very useful one, is that I have always thought I would be an MP. It's just something I always knew I would do, and I knew I wouldn't be satisfied until I had done it. If one were being pompous – and why not? – there is also a point to be made about the difference between journalism and politics.

Journalism is a wonderful job. The most powerful post I ever had, without question, was EC correspondent of the *Daily Telegraph*, where I drew the attention of middle Britain to the inconsistencies of British government policy in Brussels. But there are two drawbacks. The first is that, as a journalist, you find it much easier to kick over someone else's sandcastle than to build your own, and that becomes wearying after a while. The second, as Douglas Hurd once said to Max Hastings, is that journalists are always on the touchline, and never on the pitch.

Let me make one thing clear. I don't want to

become an MP in order to boss people around. I want to stop them bossing me around, and, in an ideal world, I want to stop them bossing other people around.

People keep telling me, with great authority, that I will be miserable, that I will find constituency work dull, that I will disappear into a whisky bottle somewhere in the Pugin corridors of Westminster. I don't believe a word of it. To be an MP, to be asked to speak for a constituency which has elected you, gives you an unbeatable legitimacy. I long to get on with the job, to see political questions not just as subjects for a few mordant paradoxes or thunderous paragraphs, but as questions to which you might conceivably, eventually, supply part of the answer. In a conversation with Sion Simon, who is also standing this year, for Birmingham and for Labour, we agree: the people who are really mad are the people who don't want to be MPs.

And what about your wife? people ask me. How will she put up with it? Good question, I say.

We walk in and I am already squirming. He's going to say it. There's no way I can stop him. It's Henley town hall, and the master of ceremonies, bemedalled, red-tailcoated, red-faced, is pumping up his lungs to announce our entry. In vain have I tried to set him straight as we loiter outside, but he seems, perhaps as a result of shouting his head off for a living, to be deaf. Our names are written on the list of guests sitting at the top table, and I can already hear the clunking faux pas.

'Mr Boris Johnson!' raves the purple-jowled magnifico. 'And, his, ah, lady, Mzzzzz Marina Wheeler!'

Blushing, we make our entrance. This, it seems to me, is the price we pay for our frail modern conventions. Marina and I have been married for eight years. We have four children. But because she likes to keep her maiden name for professional purposes, it will sound to the people of Henley as if I am squiring some girlfriend around. Even Marina – a feminist from her tenderest years – feels a prickle of embarrassment. I make a point, during my speech later on, of explaining her status.

How pathetic, you may say, at the beginning of the twenty-first century, that a chap should worry about what people think. Relax, you may say. No one cares any more what wives are called. It's over, they tell us, all that business of being a dutiful little Tory wife. The Tories have changed their attitudes to women. Haven't they?

I'm not so sure. Of course, it was worse in the old days, when the wives were paraded on the selection platforms and interrogated by the beady-eyed homemakers. My parents both remember the moment, on some school stage in the home counties, when they turned to my mother and said, 'And tell us, Mrs Johnson, how you propose to help your husband during the campaign.'

My mother played for time. 'What do you mean by campaign?' she asked them. This was a fair response, though not, perhaps, the one they were looking for.

A couple of decades later there have been some vaguely feminist advances. There are more female MPs. Some of the old segregated bodies have faded away; mainly because women have lost interest in them. After much deliberation the body known as the Conservative Wives' Club has renamed itself the Spouses' Club, though this may be because members objected to being called Conservatives, more than they resented the word 'wife'. It has been made clear to Marina that she is not expected to turn up for orgies of chutney-making. Nor is she called upon to appear at some ladies' luncheon club where, in former times, the audience might have been treated to a paper called 'Travelling in Chianti' or 'Nothing Wrong with a Loving Smack'. That is because the ladies' luncheon club no longer exists. And yet Tories are still pretty conservative in their views of the relations between the sexes and the natural order of things.

There is evidence that constituency associations – especially the female members – are biased against women. Gill Andrews, it seemed to me, scored quite a few more boundaries than us during our question-and-answer session; yet she came last. On the same night it was clear that my single greatest advantage over David Platt was that I had a wife, beaming up at me from the front row, with every appearance of interest, and wearing a suitably colourful flowery coat. And that, more or less, is where the Tories still seem to imagine a woman should be: gazing with frank adoration at her pin-striped hero.

Well, as Peta Buscombe pointed out in a recent edition of the *Spectator*, it's all over, folks. Ils sont passés, ces beaux jours. Somehow the chicks are no longer turned on by the prospect of being allowed to straighten the candidate's tie or brush aside his boyish forelock. According to Peta, there are hardly any female members of the Tory party under forty-five – fewer than 2 per cent. And no wonder, when candidates for the leadership of the party can say, in the deathless words of Ken Clarke, 'We must reach out to women – and the Welsh!'

Iain Duncan Smith was not to be outdone in this effort to embrace a kinder, gentler politics. He called upon his party to 'speak in a language that women can understand'. That is the sort of thing, says Baroness Buscombe, that drives the modern woman away, and she speaks as a former Conservative vice-chairman with responsibility for women. The Tories, she says, in her painful article, have a 'problem with women'. There can hardly be any Tory man, or indeed any man, who would not have to put his hand up, occasionally, to that one. The question is how to solve the problem.

Labour has gone for all-women shortlists, which produced more than a hundred female Labour MPs. These 'Blair's babes' have received mixed reviews as legislators. Anyway, such lists are a thoroughly bad idea, because they replace informal discrimination with formal discrimination. If applied in the Tory party, they would provoke endless resentment and, no doubt, litigation, in which sulky young men in suits hired Cherie Booth to vindicate their human rights.

A better answer, perhaps, is for the Tories to become more generally attractive to human beings of either sex, and not just attractive to women. They are very busy, these women of whom Peta Buscombe speaks, with their jobs and their families. They want to hear something snappy from a party that has a prospect of power, and knows where it is going. That means that the Tories should talk less about themselves (for which read discussions on 'Europe') and more about what they can do for the country.

So whenever I can, I try to talk about health, education, crime, in the perhaps naïve belief that these are women's issues. And quite often, of course, it is a woman who puts her hand up, and says, 'Now, Mr Johnson, that's enough on toast: what have you got to say about the European Convention on Human Rights?'

Here's my idea of the political holy grail. It will go to the first politician who can talk sense about how to make it easier for women to work and have a family, without offending (a) the women who are content just to bring up children; or (b) the women who merely have jobs; or (c) the women who have neither.

I can already hear the protests: Did he say 'Just have children'? 'Merely have jobs'? Just! Just! Merely! The first man to work that one out gets the coconut. Or the first woman, of course.

Europe

Sunday 13 May

One of the conventions of British elections is that the favourite does not consent to debate with his challengers. They need the publicity, runs the argument, and you don't. So don't bother, said Chris, who is always right. An exception is generally made in the case of the debates run by the local churches. These are, I suppose, intended to be less party-political, and to expose the positions of the candidates on issues which may not appear in party manifestos, but which might be very important to some electors.

Everything goes OK at this particular gig, at a church hall in Henley. I think I have the measure of Janet Matthews, the very nice Labour candidate who lives in Shiplake, and Catherine Bearder of the Lib Dems. I have reckoned without Oliver Tickell, the bearded, booming, bespectacled candidate of the

Green Party. The point about Oliver is that he can talk the hind leg off a donkey. If I were a donkey, and I saw Oliver walk into a church hall, I would keep my back to the wall in sheer terror.

He does not so much answer questions as deliver great Ciceronian periods, stuffed full of reflections on biology and economic theory, with comments on human nature gleaned from observation of his new-born child. After a while I am feeling a bit wan and flattened, and my answers really seem anaemic next to his. But I have known Oliver for years. In fact, I remember him from a childhood skiing expedition, and he gave us, one suppertime, a volcanic speech about quantum physics. I try to tease him about his anti-free-trade views.

Much to the audience's approval, he seems to be arguing for UK autarky, and an end to the pointless traffic in goods between nations. Oh come on, Oliver, I say, what about the banana? Are you telling the people of Henley that when you come to power, you will deprive them of bananas?

But Oliver has a brilliant answer, taking in the Windward Islands and the Leeward Islands, and the struggling peons of Latin America, where the infamous 'dollar' bananas are produced by Dole and Chiquita, which was once the United Fruit Company and a well-known front for the CIA ... etc. etc. And it is in answer to the next question, when I am already reeling, that Oliver delivers the knock-out blow.

At the beginning of the debate we have all explained that we have homes in the area, and I have described my rented accommodation in Swyncombe. Now, in answer to a question about education (Would you use state schools?) I say that my children are in a state primary in Islington.

At which point Oliver pipes up, quick as a flash, and says he hopes I have a good eco-friendly way of taking the children to school every morning, since it is a round trip of about 100 miles from Swyncombe to Islington. Huge guffaws. Game, set and match to Tickell – or Ovular, as we used to call him.

Before the debate, we are all given a sheet listing the questions people are likely to ask. You may or may not be surprised to hear that ten out of eighteen concern Europe. When, oh when, will the Tories stop picking this scab?

From the outset of this operation, I have experienced invidious comparisons with the sitting MP for Henley. Would I be an orator to match Hezza? Were the people of Henley wise to replace such a snappy dresser with a man in stumblebum suits? Where would I live, and would it be up to Château Heseltine? And what about our widely diverging views on the issue that has kept the Tories scratching for the last ten years?

* * *

Oh ho, said my friend and colleague Frank Johnson when told about my attempt to be selected for Henley, and what will Mr Heseltine make of that, eh? Hmm, he said, the Heselteenies won't like it at all. And instantly he began to imagine the battle plan of the Europhiles. 'They'll try and stop you, old son,' warned Frank. 'You must be on your guard.'

He seemed to have a point. Had I not been described in the press as a 'hardline Euro-sceptic', a 'Brussels-basher', a 'Europhobe'? Had I not exposed the plan to build a single European condom? Someone suggested that my very presence on the shortlist was another attempt at Thatcherian revenge on Tarzan, for defenestrating her in 1990. Watch out, said Frank, and began to map out how the forces of Europhoria would defend Henley: this pepperpot is Garel-Jones; the mustard is Geoffrey Howe; the spoon is Leon Brittan. They were all converging on the ancient town, represented by his place-mat, with a view to repelling the sceptic onslaught (in the form of the pint pot? The great British banger?). Well, I don't know if there was any serious effort by allies of Michael Heseltine to interfere with the selection, but I doubt it. As for Hezza, he was far too dignified – and too fly – to get involved.

We went on the *Today* programme, he and I, the

morning after the final round; and he was superb in his flattery. He said we were 'like two peas in a pod', and that he was sure the selectors had done wisely; and his successor preened desperately. Just fancy! Old Hezza, saying I was all right, after all that sarcastic stuff we used to write in the *Spectator* about his hair, and his enthusiasm for the European Space Agency and putting a Frenchman sur la lune. And over the next few months I have to admit that I came to like Michael Heseltine. Partly this is because of my natural Tory-boy deference to one of the big figures in post-war politics. He was the flogger of the council houses, the proconsul sent by Thatcher to run Liverpool, the Curzon of the Scousers. He was the Cold War Defence Secretary who, in the 1980s, could move the women of Greenham Common and the Tory conference to alternate ululations of hatred and sexual rapture. He also strikes me as being less aloof, funnier and more curious about other people than you may have been led to believe. And above all, he was and is unremittingly kind to me, which, in my book, is almost all that counts. If he experienced a spasm at being succeeded by an arch-sceptic, he mastered it magnificently.

By October 2000, when we spoke together at the Spread Eagle in Thame, we were getting on pretty well. Hezza made a joke about how 'I hope to live to a great old age, Mr Chairman, when I will be able to watch Boris, as Prime Minister, take Britain into the single European currency.' This at once boosted my ego and belittled my Euro-scepticism.

I replied with some stuff about what a hard act Hezza was to follow. 'I don't know if you've ever seen a Walt Disney film, ladies and gentlemen, called *The Lion King*. It has the same plot as *Hamlet* (nods, groans, etc.). Anyway, there is a poignant moment when Simba the cub realises he must succeed Mufasa, the bushy-maned king of the veld. And as he's following the great beast one day, he comes upon his enormous paw-print, and compares it with his own tiny pug-mark; and that is very much the spirit in which I address you tonight, goggling at the vast footprints this man has left across the British political landscape' (passing of sick-bags all round).

I have now used this little simile quite a few times, and Marina is familiar with it to the point where it has an emetic effect (rivalled only by the story about the toast). Even Hezza, who might have been quite pleased, seems to think it chunderous. 'Oh no,' he said, when I told him that in accordance with convention my maiden speech had praised the previous member; 'not that ghastly lion business again.' In fact, the general level of chumminess with Hezza has caused some tut-tutting. One gossip column suggested that there was a 'deal' between Hezza and his successor; he would call off the Heselteenies, allow me to win Henley, and I would back Ken Clarke for the Tory leadership. This is an interesting idea, but total balls.

Worse followed. An enraged Brugeiste said that Mr Johnson had lost all credibility as a Euro-sceptic. That is not something we Euro-sceptics can afford to take lying down. We do not like to have our Euro-sceptic machismo impugned. Where was the Brugeiste when Britain left the ERM? Did he uncover the plan for a Euro-coffin? Did he ever write a path-breaking article called 'Delors Plan to Rule Europe', so marrow-freezingly Euro-sceptic that it caused the Danes, on that holy day of 2 June 1992, to throw out the Maastricht Treaty? Let me try to silence the vain bibble-babble of him and his kind.

You can be perfectly friendly with people you disagree with, and my cordiality with Hezza in no way diminishes my basic Euro-scepticism. Michael Heseltine recently told the *Spectator* that Britain would one day be so seamlessly woven into the single European polity that the very name would be forgotten. Britain, he prophesied, would become as ossified a concept as Mercia or Wessex. In so far as Michael Heseltine believes this, his views are plainly barmy. It is hard to psychoanalyse this kind of Europhilia, but it has always struck me as having something to do with an irrational hostility to America. Sometimes – though I do not suggest this in Heseltine's case – it is also linked to a cynical impatience with one's own country.

I was recently waiting for some chips in a seaside tavern in Devon with my brother-in-law, Ivo Dawnay, and when, after forty minutes, the chips were still not there, Ivo launched into a fiery attack on British waitressing, culture, economic habits and all the rest. 'And that's why,' he concluded, 'we should just shut up and allow ourselves to be integrated into Europe. Christ, man, the Portuguese are better than us at this kind of thing. We need the Europeans to teach us a lesson.'

Well, we all feel like that from time to time, when the chips are down, or absent; but you don't believe, surely, that you can improve the standards of waitressing in Woolacombe by demolishing a thousand years of British parliamentary democracy? Do you? Perhaps you do.

It is a chronic vice of the British middle classes to think that their country would be better off run, in Auberon Waugh's phrase, by a 'junta of Belgian ticket inspectors'. That is, in my view, a delusion, and I say that not just because I have some knowledge of Belgian ticket inspectors.

After I had been reporting from Brussels for a couple of years, Max Hastings called me in to see him at Telegraph Towers. 'Good stuff, good stuff,' he said;

'but I don't want you turning into one of those Eurosceptics, like Charles Moore.'

B-but, Max, I said, you don't know what I'm up against. The whole thing seemed to me, and still does, a repetitive humiliation of British democracy. I remember the tone of voice, when I ran her to earth, of the Brussels bureaucrat who was responsible for drawing up the edict outlawing the prawn cocktail flavour crisp. Someone somewhere had made some mammals eat quantities of prawn cocktail flavour crisps, and concluded that they could cause hyperactivity in children. As it happens, even our own nannyish Department of Health disagreed. Nonsense, said British health experts. As part of the balanced diet of a British child – 2 packs Quavers, 3 chocolate Magnums, 2 oz dogshit per day – the prawn cocktail flavour crisp was thoroughly nutritious. The problem, as ever, was that British crisps could in theory be sold across the entire single market, and the question was therefore one for a qualified majority vote. Britain could be overruled. 'Look,' I said to the woman in Directorate-General Five (Internal Market) – and if I was testy that is because all war-zone reporters eventually become engaged with the story – 'what business is it of yours?'

'It doesn't matter,' she snapped back. 'It's not good for children to eat all those crisps.'

What I hated about Brussels was not just our national impotence, but the lying, our lying. Thatcher's ministers, and Major's ministers, and now Blair's ministers, would come out to Brussels, and do a little drum roll about how they were going to fight, fight, and fight again to stave off some directive or regulation. And then, having fought them on the beaches, and on the landing-grounds, and in the fields and in the streets, and in the hills, the men from Ukrep would cheerfully surrender. Because it would turn out that this was not, in fact, some invincible point of national pride. It was just another chip to be used in the endless all-night casino of EU negotiations. It was all fungible. It was all up for grabs. Matters of national policy, agreed on in cabinet and therefore bearing the stamp of British democratic approval, were just part of our negotiating capital.

Many of us moderate Euro-sceptics have spent our nights tossing and turning, and wondering whether we can credibly argue for staying in the EU. (Others may be kept awake by more exciting things, but that is what we are like, we Euro-sceptics. We are devoted to our subject.) Sometimes, in those bleak vigils, it has seemed that there is no answer to Norman Lamont, who is in favour of getting out. The British economy would not collapse – far from it; some sectors might experience some small improvement. But what always just about clinches it for me is that we would lose influence in the designing of the continent. And it has been the object of 500 years of British diplomacy to ensure that continental Europe is not united against our interests. It is also possible that the move would encourage a certain meanness in the national outlook; though others might think that a price worth paying.

This trade-off was well summed up, for me, by a nice middle-aged Dutch couple I met while on the campaign trail in Kidmore End. They were trying to sell me their house, a 1720 creation, rich in inglenooks and antimacassars, though pretty generously priced (In matters of commerce the fault of the Dutch/Is offering too little and asking too much). They were going back to Holland after twenty-eight years because the husband had contracted multiple sclerosis; and there was an elegiac flavour to his opinions of England, and the Tory party. He was a clever man, who had done a degree in history after his retirement from the chemical industry, and his intelligence showed in his brown, probing eyes. Suddenly, in the quiet of their sitting room, we started having an argument.

The Tories had become too extreme, he said; they were out of touch with middle England. Full of mulled wine from a pre-lunch party, I repeated the points about democracy. They were unimpressed. 'It's like when a family goes on holiday,' said the man. 'One group wants to go to the mountains, and another group wants to go to the seaside, and so you must compromise.'

But the EU is not like a family, I protested. It doesn't command the same automatic allegiance of its members. What do you say to the British electorate, when their politicians are outvoted in Brussels?

'What have the British been outvoted on?' he asked, and his eyes bored into mine.

Well, I blustered, momentarily forgetting my texts ... the ... er ... the forty-eight-hour week, for instance. What do you say to that?

'You win some, you lose some,' he said.

Indeed. My only question is whether you have to lose quite so many.

A pamphlet on something called 'Mainstream Conservatism' has swum to the surface of my desk. It appears to be written by various Europhile Tories of the old school, and the passage on Brussels is so goody-goody that it could have been from the pen of Fotherington-Thomas. 'The proper pursuit of our national interest should not blind us to the fact that other countries have their interests, too, and these should be treated with sensitivity and respect.' Tell that to the French. Tell that to the Spanish. I accept the need to be there, in Brussels, to keep our seat at the table, to retain 'influence'. What I do not accept is the continuing Foreign Office assertion that the only way to maintain our influence is to give way. It's absurd. It's like saying that the only way we can get what we want in Brussels is to do exactly as we are told.

This was my message, then, of tough, pragmatic, moderate Euro-scepticism, one cold wet night in Henley town hall, in a debate against Keith Vaz, the Minister for Europe. A good deal has been written in dispraise of Mr Vaz. All the newspapers seem to agree that he is a slippery customer. As the election approached, he became a synonym for sleaze, his very name mocked for its lubricant connotations. Vaz, said the papers, was part of the 'Asian' culture, in which it was thought quite normal, goodness gracious me, for portly, ghee-fed politicians to be in the pay of portly, ghee-fed businessmen. I hope you won't think me perverse, but it struck me that he was hard done by. Tell me, all you who think he is as greasy as an onion bhaji, exactly what he is supposed to have done. Can you formulate, in one sentence, the charge against Nigel Keith Vaz? I thought not. Whatever they say about him, he had the effrontery to turn up at a public meeting in Henley and defend the government's position on Europe, and for that I am in his debt.

He tried to explain why it was necessary to concede more qualified majority voting at the Nice summit. He tried to substantiate the claim that the Nice Treaty was 'necessary for enlargement' (utter nonsense: if the member states really wanted to expedite enlargement, they would convene an inter-governmental conference, and get on with it). It was him against me, with Terry Buckett of the Residents' Group a stone Buddha of impartiality in the chair. Though I say it myself, I reckon Vaz received the kind of thrashing that a squash ball gets at the hands of Jahangir Khan, and he was soon bouncing all over the panelled walls of the upper chamber. No one, however, could pretend that this was thanks to my own forensic skills.

Vaz was in the lion's den, with an audience of about 200, almost all of whom were Euro-sceptics. His entrance to the hall was picketed by fierce-looking men with flyers saying VAZ WASHES WHITER! He was asking for it, and he got it. David Orpwood the pig farmer gave him a decibelic denunciation of Brussels and its agricultural policy, which left him looking particularly shell-shocked. At the end of the evening I was privately hugging myself with satisfaction. I hugged too soon.

Just as we were leaving, Vaz had signalled to one of the Foreign Office gofers, who produced a funny framed certificate. It is still on my table at the *Spectator*, and it reads, 'To mark the Occasion of the Europe debate at Henley-on-Thames, 16 December 2000, Boris Johnson has been accorded the title of CHAMPION FOR EUROPE. Signed, Keith Vaz, Minister of State, Foreign and Commonwealth Office.' A nice satirical touch, I thought, and forgot about it.

I underestimated the wiliness of Vaz. Assorted other Foreign Office gofers (there were about five of them there, all at the taxpayers' expense) had taken a photo of the presentation. Weeks later this turned up in some appalling and mendacious Foreign Office 'Euro-newsletter' as a kind of heart-warming good news story. VAZ MAKES BORIS CHAMPION OF EUROPE, said the headline, suggesting that this was an event as marvellous as St Paul winning a barbarian satrap for Christ. For months afterwards I received cross letters from disappointed readers, wanting to know what the hell I was playing at. Nice one, Vaz.

As for the Euro-sceptics, do you think I won them to my cause by my trenchant performance? In some cases, I hope so, since I believe (obviously) that my position is the best for the country and for the EU. But for the hard cases, the purists, the men of Bruges, the get-outers, I was about as much use as a chocolate teapot.

It seems that UKIP, the United Kingdom Independence Party, briefly wondered whether or not to stand against me, since I had a good record of Brusselsbashing. In my cowardly way I hoped they would lay off, since they might well cost me a few thousand votes. They did not debate for long. They found a candidate, articulate, solid, with an excellent cv, and soon the armies of UKIP were to be seen marching through the Henley farmers' market with their purple and yellow banners. As the corn started to ripen in the fields the following year, garish UKIP posters sprouted on the verges. I always felt sad when I saw them, because the UKIP people thought like me, and they were almost all former Tories.

Come on, I begged one of them, canvassing one afternoon in Nettlebed. Don't waste your vote. You know the Tories are the only party who can deliver a proper Euro-sceptic government. He was a rangy, red-faced, weather-beaten man in jeans, and I remember his cackle as he took one of our stickers with my name on it. 'I'll wear it here,' he said, slapping it on the seat of his pants, 'and I'll blow it off when I fart.'

And he stalked off, with my name bobbing upside down on his arse. That's what the proper Euro-sceptics thought of me. And the proper Europhiles continued to think I was a monster who wanted to cut Britain adrift.

A Few Ill-chosen Words

'And now,' said the Mayor of Henley, in that moment we all dread, 'I call upon our guest speaker,' and there was nothing for it. It was one of the most important and potentially the trickiest speeches of the campaign. It was the Mayor's banquet.

The Mayor of Henley is a magnificent figure. His raven hair is swept back, he has an imperial nose, and always, whenever he is in public view, the great chain of office hangs richly about his neck. His liveried black limo and chauffeur dawdle for him outside the town hall, and, for all that, he retains his intimate links with the people of Henley, who have elected him no fewer than twelve times in the last thirty years.

Tony Lane is an artisan. He still runs his cobbler's shop in a back street, and to his door still comes a stream of people bearing shoes which he will repair according to inveterate principles. Around him is a scene of Dickensian industry, which really ought to be imagined in sepia. There are mounds of decommissioned pumps and brogues and Oxfords and loafers, of a fashionability one might expect from a town like Henley. The atmosphere is full of leather dust. There are about half a dozen sewing machines of almost unbelievable antiquity, all of which Tony can still operate, and there is a telephone.

That telephone is one of the hubs of Henley politics, and anyone who has studied the pages of the *Henley Standard* will know how well he uses it. Tony Lane is also a man of great charm, and it was a kindness to give me this opportunity to impress. Which is why I was nervous as I stood up, and the crowd fell silent, the Deputy Lord Lieutenant and the assorted leaders of Henley society. We were celebrating the hundredth anniversary of the construction of the town hall, which was itself built to celebrate the sixtieth anniversary of Victoria's accession to the throne. To save you consulting Pevsner, the exterior has a delightful entablature of the royal arms, carved in biscuit-coloured stone. The upper room is a masterpiece with wedding-cake white plaster moulding, offset, in a Wedgwood sort of way, with blue paint. All evening an organist had played a medley of patriotic songs, and now I was required to sing of Henley. But sing what, eh, Muse?

One problem of the battle for Henley was that I was following a famous Tory orator. You can buy tapes of Hezza saying in 1982 that Michael Foot was leading a one-legged army, 'Left, Left, Left,' and you can hear the Tory conference virtually ovulating in the background. I remember weeping at one conference, in those far-off days when the Tories were in power, when he said he had recently read a speech by the Shadow Chancellor Gordon Brown, which contained the phrase 'neo-classical endogenous growth theory'. Upon making enquiries Heseltine discovered that it was not written by the Shadow Chancellor himself but by a teenage scribbler called Mr Ball.

'So there you have it, Mr Chairman,' said Hezza to an audience already incontinent with pleasure because they could see the punchline. 'It wasn't Brown's; it was Balls!'

In one sense the political speech is a mystifying survivor from the classical education. Poetry has more or less had it. Nobody reads it, though we all write it. Theatre is a fossilised relic. But of all the ancient arts, oratory is still practised – to an almost alarming degree.

People still turn out, when they could be watching TV, to hear the human voice raised in sustained athletic effort. Sane men and women will pay for after-dinner speeches, when they could be just as amused by reading a few pages of a newspaper. In modern politics it is customary to try to disguise the formality of the genre by referring to what is to follow as 'saying a few words'. The chap always says, 'I am now going to call upon so and so to say a few words,' and then for an anarchic moment you think, Which words shall I say – Hottentot? Axolotl? Carminative? – and how few can I get away with? But you know that 'a few' always means fifteen minutes, and sometimes your host leaves you with no way out. He or she beams at you and says, 'I now call on Mr Johnson to say a few *well chosen* words.'

My confidence as a public speaker has increased, from a low base, by trial and error. You can have some brilliant philippic prepared, and it will have them all coughing and scratching and yawning or – worse – heckling. You must have a sense of your audience and, as I learned during the battle for Clwyd South, it is easy to get the mood wrong.

Some have 'Nam flashbacks. Some dream they are late for their final papers in philosophical logic and cannot find their gown. Some dream their teeth are falling out, or that they are about to be executed with a scimitar by a beautiful black woman (I have this quite often, actually). I dream I am giving a speech during the 1997 election. I had just been picked as the candidate for Clwyd South, and the area in which

I was speaking was the Wrexham Maelor, a lush salient of Wales projecting into Shropshire, which has one of the highest concentrations of cattle in western Europe.

As I drove up the M6 it hit me. Aha, I thought, I'll give them a speech about BSE. It was early 1996; the crisis was at its peak. John Major's government had had enough of being pushed around in the Brussels playground, and decided to launch the beef war. It was the perfect subject: a bit of politics, a bit of farming, a bit of Europe. The Maelor's folk were crushing into the Hanmer Arms. There were tall aristocrats in tweeds – in fact, there were the Hanmers themselves, I think – and farmers with their hands that make us ashamed of our softness, worked so hard that the nails are just little discs on the end of the fingers. And there were people my age whom I especially wanted to impress.

So I gave them a polished account of the crisis so far, drawing heavily on a column I had written (CRY HAVOC AND LET SLIP THE COWS OF WAR), heaping derision on Labour, and on the credulity of the consumer, and studding my remarks with words like hecatomb (the slaughter of 100 oxen) and holocaust (the burning of all parts of a sacrificial animal). Come on: be merciful – when else do you get to use these words in their proper sense, in a modern context?

And at first, as I ventilated my little jeux d'esprit, it seemed that things were going well. There had been some mishandling of the media – not so much a case of a mad cow, ladies and gentlemen, as a bum steer ho ho ho – and there were one or two who seemed to appreciate that kind of thing. But about halfway through I became aware of a silence from the farmers at the back of the hall. They were not thudding their tables. They were not rolling around. I ploughed on until, conscious of the first prickings of perspiration, I sat down. There was perfunctory applause, and then questions.

The first couple were OK, but then I noticed a posh-looking chap in a hairy Prince of Wales suit who was dying to get something off his chest. 'This isn't a question,' he said. 'It's more of an observation. I just think our speaker ought to realise that this crisis isn't a laughing matter, and that it's a damn serious business for a lot of the people in this room.'

I wasn't so much crushed as steam-hammered. I felt like those pictures of the Russians who got in the way of the Panzers on day one of Barbarossa. That was one of my first and most searing lessons in the difference between punditry and politics, between what makes a good leader page article and the necessities of a political speech. I hated myself in that instance for not having the imagination to see that people's livelihoods were at stake. They must have thought it bizarre to come up from London and strike a load of mordant paradoxes about BSE. It wasn't that my speech was irrelevant, or that the points were ill-founded. It was the tone. It wasn't the speech of a man who might be able to help, but of a cynical spectator. Think about their position. Under the EU treaty they were forbidden from exporting their beef to other EU countries and even to the rest of the world. Their incomes had collapsed. They wanted me to sound as if I had some practical understanding of farming and its difficulties. Which I think I had, but I gave no sign of it that night.

So thanks to the chap in the tweed suit – I think he was a colonel of some description. It was like a horrible talking-to from a teacher, of a kind you never forget because you know the bastard is, essentially, right.

Just remember. Sometimes they want jokes. Sometimes they want to get serious. Sometimes they want philosophy, and sometimes they just want Labour-bashing. But all the time, without exception, they seem to want Ann Widdecombe. How many times have I sat at a dinner and been told that Ann was there a few months ago, and everyone sort of quivers dithyrambically at the memory. Oh yes? you say, toying miserably with your chicken. Oooh yeees, they say. She was brilliant, and then they look at you, and tell you that they have a friend who once read one of your articles but they are *Times* readers themselves.

Pity us, then, who are so unfortunate as to speak to audiences who have known the ecstasy of Widdecombe. I imagine it is like being asked to make love to a woman who has just achieved bliss in the arms of Errol Flynn, or Robin Cook, or someone.

So there I was, already bruised, as a speechmaker, by the experience of following the Blue Nun, and now bobbing in the wake of Hezza. And to make matters worse, I had already had one disaster in this very room a few weeks ago. It was a speech at a ball for the National Childbirth Trust; or to be more accurate, I had a long speech prepared, full of winsome gags about childbirth. But somehow or other it failed to penetrate the audience that someone was speaking to them. They concentrated on talking to their neighbours. I tried talking louder in the hope of catching their attention. They just talked louder themselves, until I sat down in a state of more or less total humiliation, after discharging one twentieth of my oration, and had a drink.

But it is by suffering that we learn. The Childbirth Trust debacle had taught me a lesson about the room – that it has bad acoustics. And as I rose for the second time, I remembered a rule: if you are losing them, don't speak louder or faster. Speak slower, like Alistair Cooke. Make them wait for it. In fact, perhaps the reader will not mind if I now share a few of my top tips for these events, the things I have learned during an inglorious career as a public speaker.

1. *Turn Up.* May I continue my abject grovelling to the Taunton Conservative Association, who recently sold a lot of tickets for 'An Evening with Boris Johnson', while Boris Johnson was having an evening with the TV. As it was, the candidate, Adrian Flook, had to do the speech himself. He was the chap who ousted the anti-hunting Lib Dem Jackie Ballard, and provided one of the few truly joyous moments of 7–8 June, so it does not look as though my absence was electorally decisive.

2. *Remember Where You Are.* I have every sympathy with Ronald Reagan, who used to say how pleased he was to be in Colombia when he was in fact in Peru. Establish the name of the local MP. Fix it in your head.

3. *The Raffle.* If you keep picking the low numbers, or the blue tickets rather than the white tickets, people can become cross. At one event a woman in the front row started drumming her feet and shouting, 'Charlie Kennedy, Charlie Kennedy.' In an effort to show how hard I was trying to produce an impartial result, we spun the urn too hard, and it came off its moorings

with a great crash. By the way, do not even think of winning the raffle yourself, as I did at a Henley Rugby Club lunch. I won a huge box of After Eights, and made the mistake of not immediately giving them back. That is the kind of thing people neither forget nor forgive.

4. *Bad Jokes Lose Votes*. In a hotly contested field, the worst joke I have ever made was at a wonderful summer barbecue given by Jean Gladstone in the village of Benson. Madness took me over, and I said something about the hedges of Benson, or about Benson and its hedges. One man wrote to me after the election to say he had voted Liberal Democrat on the strength of that remark alone.

5. Which brings me lastly to *Alcohol*. The first thing to remember, when you have your first glass of Bolivian Cabernet, is whether or not you have drunk at lunchtime. If you are already sunk in gloom because the audience is expecting Ann Widdecombe, you may find that alcohol produces the opposite of elation. In fact, you can get a sudden chemical blackness, which can make for an unsettling speech. Even if you have not drunk at lunchtime, there is a difference between two glasses of Paraguayan Merlot and three.

On two glasses you can still be fairly terse, but after three you can find yourself having that weird out-of-body experience. Your words become detached from their meaning. You have them on your notes in front of you, but what is it all about? You try going fast or slow to see if they make any more sense, and your audience looks at you with ever more perplexity. After one such debacle I got a note from the kind woman who organised the gig, beginning: 'You are naughty …'

Readers may think it weak of me to admit all this, but don't forget how nerve-racking it can be to sit and wait. Often the lay-out means that the occupants of the top table face out into the hall, with no one opposite to shield them from the general gaze.

Even if your speech goes well, things can still deteriorate. You must keep your wits about you. As it happened, I gave a reasonable speech in the town hall, and was feeling a bit of post-match euphoria, because I then let my guard down with the *Henley Standard*.

As I say, the ealdormen and members of the witenagemot of Henley were there with their massy chains of office, and there on the table in front of us was the most enormous ceremonial mace which, according to Tony Lane, dated from 1400. This allowed me to make a little joke.

'It is bad enough trying to follow Michael Heseltine, but look at the challenge you have laid on for me tonight. Who can forget how Tarzan, my predecessor, won his nickname from the awestruck parliamentary sketch writers?

'It was late one night in the Commons, and Labour had just flouted some vital procedural convention, and such was his wrath that with golden locks flying he advanced upon the nearest weapon and waved it above his head. Who can remember what served as Tarzan's club, on that infamous occasion?

'It was the mace – and here is another, a challenge to my virility. It is the most amazing mace I have ever seen. I promise you, however else I try to emulate my predecessor, I won't wave that mace. Oh no. I'm far too bashful, nervous,' etc. etc.

Go on, go on, they cried. Lift it! Swirl it! And I refused. But afterwards, in my relief at having finished the speech in one piece, I gave in to the blandishments of the media. It was Tom Boyle, the lethal operative of the *Henley Standard*, who persuaded me to lift it up. I certainly didn't brandish the thing, but it allowed the *Henley Standard* to print a picture of me looking faintly blotto and unquestionably wielding it; which, to judge by the reaction on the doorstep, did not do much to advance my election.

Still, I was at least looking smart, in the sense that the dinner was black tie. It is not every day, though, that you can get away with wearing a uniform. If there is one thing harder than learning to string a sentence together when standing up, it is trying to look the part.

Nothing Too Hairy

OK, I said to myself as I sighted the bird down the end of the gun. This time, my fine feathered friend, there is no escape. For an hour or more I had been churning the ether with lead, and it was time to put an end to my embarrassment. And yet it wasn't really my inaccuracy which was causing me shame. No one expected me to be much cop, not when it was only my second time out shooting. They knew that I was there, as much as anything else, to demonstrate that I was a fan of country sports, and could be relied upon to stick up for them against the Blair regime.

In fact, there was only one thing wrong with the scene, timeless, Brueghelian, of men with guns and dogs, standing by the edge of a wintry wood. Almost everything was perfect, as it should be: the branches black and stark against the blue sky; the breath of the dogs hanging still in the silence while we waited for the birds; the tractor and trailer at the bottom of the hill, already starting to fill up with the day's kill; the prospect of a warming draught of soup and a Kit-Kat for elevenses. There was only one blot on the immemorial Chiltern landscape, and that was me.

The last time I'd been shooting, it had been for journalistic purposes, and I was mischievously encouraged to wear the tweeds of the seventh Earl of Derby. I cannot forget my humiliation as I came down for the shooting breakfast in some posh house in Scotland, and the tall, thin, blonde girls all started to laugh. 'I'll tell you one thing about the seventh earl,' said someone, pronging a kidney from a chafing dish; 'he must have been a bit of a lard-arse, haw haw haw.' Well, I vowed, you wouldn't catch me apeing the upper classes like that, not again. Next time, I said, I would wear my own kit.

Starting from the head, I had a baseball cap lent to me by my friend and neighbour David Orpwood, pig farmer extraordinary. There was a beige linen jacket, made in France, according to the label, by Simon Casquette. This already had a vast underarm rent, caused by whipping the gun to my shoulder. There was a pair of jeans, and lastly, and most painful of all, there was a pair of sailing galoshes one size too small, which had already lamed me with blisters. It would be nice to claim that I carried this off effortlessly, like

Salvador Dali in a purple dinner jacket. But I couldn't. I felt abashed. Everyone else was irreproachably kitted out in the full tweed panoply: deerstalker or flat cap; belted tweed jacket with umpteen pockets; knitted tie; check shirt; funny little leather cartridge handbag thing; britches; socks; stout shoes or boots. And everyone else made a gallant attempt to pretend that I didn't look like a complete prat, and that my gear was really rather original. But there was no getting away from it. I didn't look the part.

The truth, of course, is that it was such a glorious day, and the struggle to hit anything was so absorbing, that it hardly mattered. As the sun went down, though, amid the euphoric exhaustion, I remember thinking to myself that if the future Member for Henley-on-Thames goes shooting, he should damn well look as though he knows his business. Michael Heseltine, I told myself, would not have been seen dead in a pair of sailing galoshes. Which set my mind turning on the question: what should a Tory MP wear these days? It is no trivial matter.

Michael Heseltine was famous for the amazing architecture of his suits: the hammer-beams of his shoulder pads, the flying buttresses of his lapels, the subtle entasis of his trousers. These days, however, the word had gone out, from no less an authority than Amanda Platell, our chief spin doctor, that the pinstripe was dead. She was fed up, we were told, of seeing a parade of Tories stretching out, Gieved and Hawked to the gills, like some musical about merchant bankers. It was time, we were told, that Tories started to look more like the people they were purporting to represent, and less like a breed apart.

But what to do?

When campaigning in Wales, I had worn, non-stop, a tweed jacket made for me by Sam the Tailor in Hong Kong. No one ever said that my appearance then was smart, but it looked vaguely OK. When the *Daily Telegraph* published some photographs of me on the trail, one reader did violently object. I can remember his letter more or less by heart.

> Sir, (he said)
> I could have saved Boris Johnson all that shoe leather tramping through Wales in search of the Tory vote, if he had simply hired me as his spin-doctor. In the first place, his head is the wrong shape. It looks as though a piece of it is missing at the back. If he had been entering a fatstock competition, I am sure his story would have been one of unrivalled success. A last thought: has he ever been fired out of a circus cannon?

Rude, certainly, but not rude about my clothes. Alas, like everything produced by the excellent Sam of Hong Kong, the jacket has long since degenerated into rags; and so I toyed, for a while, with buying another tweed jacket and trying the same routine again. The trouble was, there didn't seem many occasions in Henley which called for a jacket and tie, or 'standard change', as we used to call it at school. So when Chris Scott told me about a forthcoming rugby match, involving Henley's formidable XV, the Hawks, I seized the moment. There is a fine outfitters in Henley called Silvers, run by a pillar of the community called Tony Elliott. He had a huge array of tweed jackets, any of which seemed to be just the job for a rugby match.

'Well, Mr Johnson,' said Tony, 'you'll be wanting a forty-six rather than a forty-four – though,' he added delicately, 'you'll be losing a lot of weight during the campaign.'

We both knew this to be untrue, since electioneering involves ingesting massive quantities of beer and sandwiches, and I looked for a really capacious number. Aha, I said, finding a green thing with deafening checks and a Neanderthal Irish heaviness about it. What do you think?

Hmm, said Tony, and after a moment's reflection he spoke what I later felt to be a great profundity: 'You'll be wanting nothing too hairy for Henley, sir.'

So I rejected this Esau of a jacket in favour of a smoother number. This had an essentially ochre hue with, I think, red, black and blue checks of great taste and discretion. I wore it to the match that afternoon. No one said anything much about it, as you might expect, and everything went well. The Henley Hawks scored a memorable victory over the London Welsh, turning it around in the second half. The day was, again, very beautiful, and I remember a light aircraft rolling and looping the loop in the azure heavens.

And that was it. That was the last proper outing my tweed jacket has had, because almost everything else in an MP's life, or in a would-be MP's life, seems to call for a suit. As Seb Coe once told me (if that isn't name-dropping, I don't know what is), 'People expect their MP to be wearing a suit. You can't go wrong in a suit.'

Seb Coe may be the fastest human being ever over 800 metres, but he's in error there. You certainly can go wrong in a suit, as A. A. Gill did not forbear to point out when he followed me around. The suit in question is illustrated on the cover of this book, and from certain angles it looks all right. The trouble is that it was designed by an itinerant tailor, who came to take my measurements in my glass-sided office in Canary Wharf, when I was still assistant editor of the *Daily Telegraph*. He made me drop my daks, as they say in Australia, in full view of the assorted *Telegraph* beauties, such as Alice Thomson and Corinna Honan, who then surrounded me in the open-plan system. It may therefore have been my self-conscious jiggling that caused him to exaggerate my measurements to the point where Gill could say that 'there was room in the seat of the trousers for a brace of floating voters'. Long before these insults, it had been borne in upon me that this was not a suit of Heseltinian nattiness, and I had taken steps.

Do you, too, find yourself wishing there was no need to have your inside leg measured in public? Do you wish suits would just appear on your doorstep? I have the answer. It is mail order. There is a man called Boden, a red-faced chap who used to be in the Oppidan Wall, and who runs a mail order suit company. He sent me a blue moleskin suit in the post, and it fits, if not like a dream, then not exactly like a nightmare. It struck me that this suit majestically fulfilled the Platell criteria: it was smart, but it was casual. It was a suit, and yet it was New Tory.

I wore it extensively during the campaign, until Christopher Squires – a military man, and one of the superheroes of the South Oxfordshire Conservative Association – took me on one side. He didn't want to be the bearer of bad news, he said, but some of the retired brigadiers had seen me canvassing outside Waitrose, and they had never seen such a shocking bad suit in all their lives. Worse still, the same suit had been spotted wandering around Phyllis Court, and had provoked similarly adverse reactions. Of course, said Christopher, he'd told them all to get stuffed. But I could see what he was thinking. The suit might be all right for a Bohemian existence in London, but not for Henley.

Mind you, when I did wear it in London, Peter Oborne, the political correspondent of the *Spectator*, sucked on his cigarette and said that it might be OK for the country, 'but not for the Commons'. What can you do, eh? One day, if I ever make any money, I will go grovelling to Michael Heseltine – whatever Amanda Platell says – and ask him the name of his tailor.

Let us suppose, in the meantime, that you have no trouble with clothes, or with women, and that you can more or less speak English when called upon to address a crowd. I have discovered that there is one requirement which, in many eyes, transcends even these. You must dwell, or at least have an abode, among those you hope to represent.

House-hunting

We were standing in the garden of one of those South Oxfordshire properties so beautiful, so English, so decorous that it induced feelings of scrotum-tightening envy. We were looking out at the Thames, across a garden that effortlessly contained a grassy seven-a-side football pitch, a tennis court and a swimming pool. On the other bank there was nothing but the hills and the heaving fleece of the trees. And there I was, jealously whimpering, when I became aware of a friendly face by my side. It was one of the guests at the pre-lunch drinks, where I had just been permitted to say a few words.

'So,' she said, following my gaze, 'when are you going to buy a house here, then?'

No one asked me during the general election campaign whether I was in favour of capital punishment. Nobody asked me how to simplify the tax system.

Nobody asked me how to reform the Common Agricultural Policy. But if I had a pound for everyone who asked me when, how and where I was proposing to buy a house in the constituency, I would not be a rich man. But I would be able to buy lunch for two at the Quat' Saisons, or a holiday for four in Ibiza.

All MPs should live in their constituencies, or so nearly adjacent as not to make any difference. It seems there was another age, and another attitude. Palmerston used to tell his association that he would not be coming up, because he felt it would be 'wrong to interfere with local affairs'. There is the story of a Victorian Sir Bufton Tufton, the former Tory MP for one of the Manchester seats, who used to visit once a year. He was met at the station by a brass band, and all the City Fathers would gather in the Free Trade Hall to hear his speech. In the years when Sir Bufton was unable to attend, his text would be specially typed up and distributed to a grateful populace. Those days are gone, and rightly.

How can I hope to speak for South Oxfordshire in the Commons unless I roam the streets and the pubs and the shops, week in, week out, and allow myself to be nobbled? That is why all political parties have for decades been obsessed with finding candidates who, if not local, can become pretty convincingly local as soon as possible. It is an indispensable requirement.

You can get away with carpet-bagging as a candidate. My father had some brilliantly satirical lines, when he was looking for a seat. 'I have never been to Leicester before, Mr Chairman,' he began, 'but I have been to Leicester Square.' He once told a constituency association on the Isle of Wight that he had never been there before, though he had seen it from the taffrail of the *Queen Mary*. He told an association in Dorset that his family was from Somerset, 'though when we had sheep, we used to run Dorset horn'. I was forced to tell my association that I was not a local man, but I had drunk much Henley bitter at school.

All that, though, will not do for long. If you are likely to win, you must have somewhere to live before the election. But where? Estate agents agree that South Oxfordshire is the single most expensive and desirable rural location in England, sandwiched between the M40 and the M4. Hezza may have had his vast pile, pillared, porticoed, pedimented, with an arboretum more stuffed with species than the rainforest. But the pharaonic Hezzopolis was to be found some way to the north of the constituency: in Northamptonshire, in fact. We looked more locally.

What's this in the *Henley Standard*? A flat in the middle of town going for £200,000? Not a three-bedroom flat, not a two-bedroom flat, but a one-bedroom flat. The cost of housing in South Oxfordshire is propelled by the London market, like one billiard ball hitting another. And we were ourselves part of the phenomenon: the endless wave of big-city professionals who wake up one morning and decide they can't take it any more. They migrate to the country, and they bring with them their big-city values, especially their property values. You remember the Aesop fable about the town mouse and the country mouse. The punchline is that Town Mouse decides the countryside is really rather too slow for him, and Country Mouse decides the town is frankly too scary for him, and each sticks to what he knows. That's not how it works these days.

These days Town Mouse wakes up and realises that on a sweltering July day he is going to have to take the Tube; and then there is the matter of the poor schools; and the repeated theft of his bike, and the burglary across the way, and the endless yellow police placards on the corner by the pub, asking for information on the latest stabbing or mugging.

And as he lies there, listening to the rising din of the London traffic and thinking of the polyaromatic hydrocarbons settling in his kiddies' lungs, Town Mouse has a vision. He sees a little flint-covered cottage, not far from a village green. He sees lush riparian scenes. He sees croquet, and girls in long white summer dresses. He fantasises about the little ones, in smart uniforms, spilling happily out of the local school. He dreams of cabbage whites coming through the open kitchen window, and red kites hovering in the blue empyrean. I want, thinks Town Mouse. Get me there now. At which point he leaps out of bed, beats his chest and goes to talk the matter over with his wife.

According to the Council for the Protection of Rural England, about 1700 people are fleeing the towns every week. They are true to Aesop, in the sense that these town mice never really become countrymen. Of course, they bring money, even if they are only really there to spend it at the weekend. But their single most important economic effect is to push up property prices to urban levels: which can be a disaster, and not just for impecunious journalists.

Take Doris, a buxom and genial girl I met who works in an old people's home, where I was trawling for votes. Doris and I hit it off from the start, mainly because I think she thought I was also called Doris. You don't get paid much if you work in nursing care, she explained, and it was very hard to find somewhere to live. She was squashed in with her mother, and the council said she didn't have enough 'points' to qualify for a council flat. Could she not rent somewhere? I hear you ask. Not at current prices.

This is not so much a problem of absolute

deprivation; it is deprivation caused by the ambient prosperity. What is the biggest difficulty facing the Thames Valley police force? It is recruitment. They have the money, says Sir Charles Pollard, the Chief Constable. But they can't find the human beings. To make matters worse, Sir Charles is battling against a London weighting, which means that you get £4000 extra to reflect the cost of living in the capital, and that has siphoned away some officers from Oxfordshire. And it is the same story in the hospitals, the nursing homes, the fire services, and everywhere else. The average cost of a house in Oxfordshire, in March 2001, was £158,865, while the national average was £110,570.

So there they sit, the affluent middle classes of South Oxfordshire, simultaneously glorying in the value of their property and complaining about the absence of bobbies on the beat – without seeing that there might be a connection between the two.

The town mice have arrived, and transformed the economics of the countryside, by flattening out the hierarchy of accommodation. In the city there are still upscale dwellings and downscale dwellings. But thanks to the incoming town mice, there are hardly any downscale dwellings to be found any more in the winding lanes of Oxfordshire. There may be tumble-down shacks and wonky-clapboarded barns and gape-windowed labourers' cottages. But in the hands of the right estate agent they are all worth anything up to half a million.

So what do you do about it? From the very moment I began campaigning for election, people started throwing this one at me. What we needed around here, I was told at Huntercombe Golf Club, was 'affordable' housing for 'young' people, who should preferably be 'local' and with 'families'. For some people, like my Liberal Democrat opponent, the whole issue showed how tragically misguided the Tories had been in flogging off the council houses. 'It was,' she said several times, 'an evil act.'

This struck me as strong language. The sale of the council houses liberated hundreds of thousands from an unnecessary state control. While canvassing during the election I met two couples – a statistically significant sample, in my view – who said they had voted Tory ever since they had been permitted to buy their houses, and would always vote Tory in simple gratitude for that policy. No one, except possibly the Liberal Democrats, was proposing a wholesale renationalisation of the old council housing stock; but what did that leave?

You could think again about the old system of tied houses. The Sheehy Report had led to the abandonment of the tied police houses, accommodation owned by the force for the use of young officers and their families. Was that worth 'revisiting'? I asked a meeting of the Henley Residents' Group. It was, they said, and I received some approving murmurs, until my suggestion was deservedly satirised by Terry Buckett, a former mayor of the town. 'Yeah,' he said, 'and we'll have tied post office houses for postmen, and tied fire brigade houses for firemen, and tied houses for newsagents ...' Actually, I think the trouble with the idea of the tie is that in ten or twenty years' time one can imagine some future Sheehy coming across all this fabulously valuable property in the forces' portfolio, and wondering why they don't sell it, especially since many of the young officers and their families would rather live somewhere else.

Which brings us to the solution actually being deployed, which is to build some affordable housing, and designate it specifically for the use of local people. For instance, South Oxfordshire District Council can require that, if there is a new development, it should contain a proportion of 'starter homes', and it can ensure that exceptions are made to normal planning rules to build social housing. You can see the problems already. How can you tell who is 'local'? How can you stop the market from asserting itself, as it always will, and tempting the owners eventually to achieve the real value of the property? And what, above all, do you do about the Nimbies?

I will leave this subject with two successive headlines from the *Henley Standard*. On 20 July we had: STARTER HOMES PLAN FOR THE FAIR MILE, with an enthusiastic story about the social benefits envisaged. On 27 July we had: FAIR MILE STARTER HOMES PLAN FURY – accompanied by a picture of angry, snowy-haired residents with their thumbs down. As I write, the protestors have set up a fighting fund.

But whatever happens to the starter homes in Henley's lovely Fair Mile, they aren't, alas, intended for me. As a town mouse moving to the area, I am really part of the problem; I don't deserve to be part of the solution. Which means that like everyone else we bob on the tidal swell of the market. After one embarrassing rejection, when a charming couple said we couldn't rent their outhouse because, frankly, we had too many children, we have found a lovely little cottage. It has roses, and a nearby cricket pitch, and a walk to an immemorial church. But it is rented; and we need to buy. Whatever I achieve as an MP, it will involve another mortgage.

We meet William Hague's sister Jane, who lives not far away. Call me a greaser, but she is extremely nice, and Marina liked her, too. She tells me that William has told her to tell me that he has quoted me in a speech he gave the other day. Which is a pretty high honour, eh? What on earth was it? I have been a Hague fan ever since he once briefed me on incapacity benefit, and explained in about three short paragraphs what the problem was and what he proposed to do about it. He is far abler, intellectually, than Blair. In many ways he has been dealt a rotten hand by fate. If only, like Pericles, he could be allowed to wear a hoplite helmet.

At the same party a chaplain comes up, and says repeatedly to both of us severally that if we ever feel in need of spiritual guidance we should come and see him. Oh dear. What does he know? Is there something about the lives of politicians that makes him think of temptation and despair?

Looking After Grandma

Monday 14 May

More canvassing, and yet more knock, knock, knocking on the doors of South Oxfordshire. We head for Sonning Common in Anthony de Normann's beaten-up old Sirocco. Who is Anthony de Normann? He is a public-spirited young ex-army entrepreneur who has become fed up with Blair, fed up with the government, and wants to see the Tories pick themselves up off the floor pdq. He lives with his family in Shiplake, but can organise his own time.

So he rings up Tory HQ in Watlington and offers to help Chris in any way he can. He is assigned the task of driving the candidate around. Over a couple of weeks I discover he is a thoroughly good egg, who has served all over the place.

He also has the distinction of successfully suing John Pilger, after the left-wing Aussie heart-throb wrote some total balls about him and a wholly innocent mission he happened to be on in Cambodia. I cannot disclose his military background, since it would cause an immediate D notice to be served on this book. Suffice it to say that he is versed in the ultimate secrets of counter-espionage, could kill an ox with his bare hands, and is very much the man you'd want on a tiger shoot. He is exceedingly tall, with a fierce glare, and when he senses resistance on the doorstep he says: 'Look, you don't want that man Blair to get back in, do you? Do you really?' He was a year or so above me at school, though we each have only a faint recollection of the other.

Canvassing is like going for a run, or any other activity requiring mental or physical effort. You need to psych yourself up a bit beforehand, but it is good fun once you get going. The routine is exactly as I remember it from Wales: open the latch of the little gate; march down the front path, ring bell, ding-dong, and watch as a shadowy form appears in the frosted glass.

'Good morning,' you say. 'I'm sorry to trouble you, but I wonder if I could introduce myself ...' If the conversation seems to require it, you can always say something about the garden. This is the time of year when England is most heart-breakingly lovely, and since you spend much of a general election standing waiting on doorsteps, you have time to take it in.

The lawns are shamingly perfect, as carefully tonsured as William Hague's buzzcut. There are whatnots and thingummies, and tall, ornamental poppies, their heads drooping like a bunch of Tory defeatists. There are those extraordinary blue bushes, ceanothus, with the blooms rolling and tumbling like breakers. There are wisteria, and such is the dedication of the gardeners in these parts that they grow to prodigious lengths. We found a wisteria flower in Goring which was four foot one inch long, and believe this may be a record. 'What a fantastic garden,' you say, and you mean it, when you think of your own blighted begonias and runty lawn. 'Oh it's nothing,' they reply. 'It's half-wild, really.'

Just wait here, says the nurse. Mrs Bonham Carter will be along shortly. So we wait. We are keen to see Mrs Bonham Carter. But more importantly, she is keen to see us. There is only the faintest chance of persuading her to vote Tory, since she is a member of the most distinguished Liberal family in England, and at the age of 102 it seems unlikely that she will yield to our pleas. The fact is, though, that Mrs Bonham Carter is still a big noise in the village of Sonning Common, and since she has indicated an interest in viewing the Tory candidate, he had damn well better present himself. So we stand in one of those nursing home rooms, me and my friend Jo, the chairman of the parish council, and I reflect on one of the weirdest rituals of British politics.

When I first visited an old people's home in search of votes during the battle for Clwyd South in 1997, I emerged stunned. Any parliamentary candidate will tell you the routine. You arrive at the door of some spacious house or grange, where every door has wheelchair access and special high-visibility banisters, and through the net curtains you see wraith-like figures regarding you with a frank lack of interest. Matron admits you with great friendliness and impartiality – she has done this dozens of times before. You meet the staff, who seem genuinely taken by the chance to see a proto-politician, and shake their hands, and then you meet the occupants.

You are walked through to a day room where the old folks are sitting, and I won't conceal it from you: the first couple of times I canvassed an old people's home, the experience left me wrung out and full of a non-specific guilt. Sometimes it is the smell of boiling chicken, so strong it is as if the air had been turned into a suspension of chicken-fat droplets. Sometimes it is the strange bedroom odour – not unpleasant, but like stale sheets or an unwashed pillow. Maybe it will be the sight of the daytime TV that depresses me, blurting away to itself in the middle of the room. It is not so much Carol Vorderman or Pamela Anderson, but the realisation that for most of these people it is a matter of deep indifference whether Pammi keeps her top on or not. Worse is the understanding, a split second later, that one day I too will be in the same position. Or perhaps my mood sinks at the sight of the unopened 1000-piece puzzle of Wordsworth's Dove Cottage. Is it that no one is able to piece it together, or that no one can be bothered?

'Now, everybody,' says Matron, or whoever has provided you with an entrée to this particular home, 'I want you to listen because we have a very special guest today. We've got Mr Bruce Johnson (or Norris Thomson, Horace Gimson, etc.), who is standing for the Conservative – have I got that right, dear? – for the Conservative Party.' Then, blushing deeply, you step into the middle of the room, and you make a short oration. The Tories are going to give people a better deal on their pensions, with x more for single pensioners and y more for married couples. And the rheumy blue eyes stare at you. Is that blankness, or is it perhaps a fleeting glance of calculation? What's more, you go on, the Tories are going to do more to fight crime, more to prevent elderly people from having to sell their property to finance their care. 'We'll ring-fence your assets,' you say, using the dead jargon of manifestos ('Hang on, darling, while I ring-fence my assets,' as the actress said to the bishop). And the eyes turn down again, and parchment-like hands reach out for their TV guides.

Having stammered to a halt, you go round and shake everyone by the hand. This is always popular, and it is essential not to leave anyone out. Sometimes the grip is surprisingly strong; sometimes the hand is just a vellum-wrapped bundle of kindling; but always the skin is so soft that it might have been rubbed for years with Oil of Ulay. And it is at that moment, when he or she has your attention, that you suddenly become aware of the brightness still shining through the eyes. A sentence is produced by those papery lips; and then another sentence, each perfectly grammatical, asking you to explain just what the hell makes you think you can count on his or her vote, and what are you really going to do for the constituency, hmmm?

After a while you manage to extricate yourself, and you find yourself shaking another hand, and you find a centurion who fought in, say, Burma, and who wants to tell you about it. The feeling that now overwhelms you, as you go round, is that these people were once as you are today: they were not insignificant in their own fields; they did the state some service and they know it. Whatever their station in life, they have seen a thing or two. They may have more than twenty direct descendants.

Of course, most of them will rapidly forget you and your visit. Your brightly printed literature will disappear into the midden of colour supplements on the coffee table, and never be thought of again. (There is the famous story of the MP who arrived in a nursing home, clasped an old biddy by the hand and said: 'Hello there, do you know who I am?' And she said, 'No, dearie, I am afraid I don't. But if you ask Matron, I am sure she'll tell you.') And yet after you have been round a few such homes, and discovered how the flame of human intelligence and individuality can still blaze away in these ancient bodies, you start to lose your distaste for the business. There is, on reflection, nothing really bizarre in what you are doing. These people may be old. They may be frail. But they all have votes. They all matter equally in our democracy, and they are all entitled to be wooed for their support. You may go away thinking – in a condescending way – that there is something a bit awful in the way so many of them seem to promise you their vote without seeming to know what they are doing. But how do you know that they are so innocent? How do you know that they are not really chuckling to themselves and waiting to spin the same story to the Lib Dems and the Labour lot, when they come round?

Take Mrs Bonham Carter, a woman who can remember quite clearly the outbreak of the First World

War, and who eventually shuffles into her chair. There are no flies on her. She enjoys the *Spectator*, she says, though she has always read *The Times* rather than the *Daily Telegraph* – no offence. Now then, she says, poring over my election bumf, with its strange gallery of pictures of the candidate with local farmers, local sheep, local policeman, local children, local shopkeepers and 'local people'. Why is it, she says, that the two main parties seem to attack each other so vehemently when they appear to be offering much the same thing? Ah ... Good question, I say. After about half an hour of interrogation I am dismissed, and her parting words are that she will of course be voting Liberal Democrat, but that it has been nice to meet me.

It is a good home, I think, when we are out in the breeze and the sunshine again; obviously run to very high standards by dedicated and patient professionals. And yet they have problems, all such homes. Here is a sketch of the issues. They raise the deepest moral questions about the relationship between the family and the state.

We all know that the population is getting older: in Oxfordshire the number of people aged more than eighty-five has risen by a third over the last ten years. The number of people aged eighteen to twenty-four has fallen quite sharply, reflecting perhaps not just birth rates but the cost of living in the area. You would have thought this would produce a boom in old people's homes. You would have thought there was a huge and growing market for ever more professional care. And yet, across the country, these places are closing, at a rate, according to a recent report, of 100 per month. There are difficulties of recruiting staff, not made easier in a place like South Oxfordshire by the cost of living, or (if I am allowed a party-political side-swipe) by recent employment legislation on hours of work. More fundamentally, there is the squabble over who should pay, the Department of Health, the Department of Social Security, or the family.

You will have heard of the problem of bed-blocking, by which old people are kept in beds in NHS hospitals just because the Department of Social Security will not pay for them to go into a home. Under the law of England and Wales the state will not pay for what is called 'residential care', though it does pay for nursing care. The distinction is hard to apply, but it seems to mean that the government will pay for a nurse to change your drip or your dressing; but not to put your slippers on or to give you a bath. So unless you are positively ill, with a recognised sickness, you may have financial problems. This rule seems particularly cruel when applied to patients with Alzheimer's disease.

As I understand it, the present law views

Alzheimer's as a symptom of senility, rather than a disease for which nursing care is necessary. Therefore the family of the victim must pay for 'residential care'. This is expensive. It may be £400 per week; it may be more. Many families feel a deep sense of grievance as they watch the assets of their sick, elderly relative being swallowed up; while they know of other patients, who are afflicted by other diseases, who have their care covered by the state. That sense of injustice is accentuated in England because the Scots have decided, under their devolved powers, that the state should pay for both nursing and residential care in Scotland. Since the English taxpayer subsidises the Scots to the tune of about £2 billion per year, this is a manifest inequity in the so-called United Kingdom, which will have one day to be resolved.

These grievances are as nothing, though, to the rage and despair of families who find that in order to pay for their loved one's care, they must sell his or her house. This is often the family home; the house where the children, now adult, grew up. This is also the house they hoped to inherit – in the rhapsodical phrase of John Major – as part of the 'cascade of wealth down the generations'. Now they see that asset, to which they may have a unique sentimental attachment, being sold off because their mother or grandmother has Alzheimer's rather than cancer. Now they find out, with great bitterness, that however much the state may have received in decades of national insurance contributions, it will not reciprocate in the painful last years. There is no protection from the cradle to the grave.

All politicians, from all parties, sense this anger. They have all promised to do something about it. The Tories raised the value of assets you could own, before you could be forced to sell your house, from £8000 to £16,000. And yet there are still 46,000 houses sold a year, more or less compulsorily, to pay for the cost of residential care.

In each case there may be the additional rage against a neighbour, who may have assets of just less than £16,000, who is not forced to sell his or her house, and who gets free care. It is a gross penalty against saving, and Tony Blair has called it 'an obscenity'. He is right, in a way. There is something miserable about being forced to sell your house; a hideous statement by the authorities that this is not a place you will now need, not a place to which you will be returning. It would be far better if more people were insured against the cost of their care in old age. And yet if we are to get anywhere in this argument, and think clearly about a solution, we ought to accept that there is another point of view.

This house, this precious family asset whose sale Mr Blair finds so 'obscene': what if it is simply true –

sad but true – that the old person no longer has need of it? Is it really right that the family should inherit this very valuable asset, tax-free, and not be called upon to pay for the care of their elderly relative? What that means is that the taxpayer – the hard-pressed low-income smoker and drinker, for instance – is paying for the cost of middle-class residential care, so that well-heeled middle-class children can inherit their parents' property. Is that right? Or is there not a touch of 'obscenity' about that, too, when we put it that way?

In all this argument, there is one assumption, in this country, which is never challenged. Whether you pay for it, or whether the state pays for it, no one has any doubt that the duty of looking after Grandma falls to everyone else but you. I look now at my gambolling brutes, aged two, three, six and eight, and I wonder how ruthlessly they will pack me off, as soon as I start to ramble and dribble and make even less sense. Perhaps I would be perfectly happy in a place as agreeable as the one in which we met Mrs Bonham Carter. Or perhaps not.

I merely point out how heartless our behaviour still seems to many Italians, and still more to the Indians. As for the ancient Greeks, they would have regarded it as treachery to repay the benefits of nurture in this way. Of course, I know it will all look and feel very different when I am eighty-five, and a frightful nuisance, and everyone wants to get on with their lives. And I will meekly say that I don't want to be a bother to anyone, and the place looks lovely, just like school, etc. But I wonder whether there might not be a case, sometimes, for allowing the old dodderer to moulder quietly in the corner of the room, full of years and respect, surrounded by people he still half-recognises, for a little bit longer. They make good points now and then, these old people.

In the evening we canvass Watlington with Roger Belson, the county council candidate. Roger is a tall, good-looking, highly intelligent man who was spifflicated in a car crash, and needs to be pushed in a wheelchair. We decide that I should do this, since it will give me an air of compassion, and it is good for both of us to be seen together. After about half an hour, during which we almost come a cropper twice on some big kerbs, Roger gallantly suggests that he should give me a rest.

I ring a bell. Ding-*dong*. Immediately through the pane I see the sight every candidate dreads: a sea of boiling teeth and thrashing tails and drooling tongues licking the glass in their eagerness to be at you. At length a kindly South African manages to open the door, sweating with the effort of restraining the yowling Schmausers or Dortmunders or Stuttgarters or whatever they are.

'What is your policy on dogs?' he wants to know. 'Oh, I'm pro-dog,' I say. 'Yes,' he says, 'but should a man be allowed to guard his house with dogs?' There is only one answer to that, I think, as the dogs' eyes loll towards me and their great jugular muscles bulge as they try to escape their master and give the Tory candidate a chomping he won't forget. 'He certainly should,' I say.

In which case, says the man, beaming and heaving his charges back over the threshold, you can count on my vote.

Mr Unpopular

Wednesday 16 May

Canvassing outside a school in Nettlebed. It takes a certain amount of guts, in these days of anti-paedophile hysteria, to stand outside school gates. It's probably against the Children Act, or the rules of Esther Rantzen's Childline.

But the mums don't mind, generally, provided you are quick and confident, and don't get in the way of their buggies. 'Sorry, no thanks,' they say, if they are not takers; and then the trick is to spring out of their way like a gazelle finding himself between a lioness and her cubs.

Today it is raining, and the literature is getting sodden. The mums are parked in their cars, grinning at us through the windscreens. There is nothing for it but to go from car to car, like match-sellers in India. They wind down their windows wearily, and we have some success. One woman wants to know whether I will stick up for hunting (I will). She is about the fifth person to have asked. 'My husband's a gamekeeper,' she explains.

By now the rain has done irreparable damage to the leaflets, and when I find a Euro-sceptic who thinks the Tories are too damn soft, I struggle to produce a KEEP THE POUND flyer. As I pull them out of the rubber band they all disintegrate, in a hideous metaphor for our policy, and thud in the swirling gutter.

Here's what I think is happening, based on talking to a hundred people or so over the last few days. It is my personal huncho-swingometer, and it has worked well in the past. I remember in 1997 ringing Charles Moore from Wales, after only a few days' campaigning, and saying we were done for. As far as I could tell, I reported, about 10 per cent of Tories were switching straight across to New Labour: which meant that a massacre impended. I was right.

This time it feels different. There isn't the same hostility to the Tories; but nor is there any particular enthusiasm for us, and there certainly isn't enough hostility towards the government. I'd say about two or three in ten of those we lost in 1997 are trickling back – that's the good news. The bad news is that the Tory vote is still a bit soft, and there are plenty of people who voted Tory in 1997 who are wondering about it this time.

My impression is that the two lots – switchers back and away – will just about cancel each other out. This means that we are due for another massacre, except at the hands of slightly different people.

The brute problem is that there are too many people who are still disillusioned with the Tories; and there are too many people who bought the shiny £19.99 New Labour toy in 1997, and are agreeably surprised to find it hasn't packed up yet.

They will come back to us, especially if there is an economic downturn, and some of Labour's new reforms appear short-sighted, and the paint starts to flake off Tony. But they will only come back if the Tories are seen, once again, as a big, broad, honest party, confident of running the country well, and more interested in talking about the electorate than about themselves.

One man who certainly isn't going to vote for us comes out of a house in Goring. He spots me and throws the keys of his car to his girlfriend, a tough-looking blonde girl. 'Go aaarn!' he shouts. 'Go and run them over.'

It is curious, the effect of TV, if you are an electoral candidate. It makes people sure they know you, and their reactions to you become rather personal, and often deluded. Aha, a man said to me recently on the Eurostar – Dorking Rugby Club, wasn't it? You were the second-row chap, weren't you? I know, said another man, after walking round me for a while at the check-in at Zaventem airport, and staring at me in a baffled way, you were staying with the McAlisters in Northumberland. Come on, yes you were. I never forget a face.

You can try saying that you've never been near Dorking Rugby Club, and that the McAlisters may have had a rip-roaring house party, but not one involving you. It makes no difference. The magic of television has convinced them; and this, of course, has its nice side as well. We were walking through Trafalgar Square not long ago and a policeman approached. I flinched, as one does, and tried to think which by-law I was then most in breach of ... The parking tickets ... The vehicle licence ... The council tax ...

'Excuse me, sir,' said the policeman, 'but could I have your autograph?'

I was stunned, and Marina almost passed out. The shaming truth is that a lot of people are very kind to me in public and say they want to shake my hand, or that they enjoy my writing, and that they hope I will continue to 'speak my mind' on TV.

I will not hide it from you, folks. I am an absolute

glutton for this sort of thing. I lap it up. I cannot get enough. But there is, of course, another dimension to becoming, if not famous, then tolerably well-known to people who accidentally watch late-night political programmes.

The other day I was off for my run, or totter, hunched against the rain, and feeling pretty low about life, the Tory party and everything, when I passed three youths. 'Oi,' said one of them as I staggered by, 'it's that c★★★ Boris.'

Heaven knows why, but this sparked feelings of aggression in me. I turned and pursued them down the pavement. 'Hey, you, ★★★★,' I said, 'why are you calling me a ★★★★?' It may be that my arms were swinging a bit, like the boxer Rocky on one of his training runs; and one of them started to imitate me as they stood there waiting for me to arrive, shadow-punching and rolling his shoulders. They seemed quite young (so does everyone these days), and had evidently just been to watch Arsenal. As I closed in, I tried to think of something really crushing to say, and I am afraid that I failed.

So I just said: 'Look, I am just off for my run, and things are bad enough, and now you call me a ★★★★. Why do you say that?'

One of them put his arm round my shoulder. Now listen, he said, it was a point in my favour that I was going for a run. But the fact was that he had seen me on TV, and formed the impression that I was a ****.

'Yeah,' said his two companions. 'You've got to face the fact that you're a ****,' one of them added, and that seemed to close the matter.

'Right,' I said, and we parted, they to their pub or club up the Holloway Road, me to my totter round the park; and as I ran I tried to work out which TV programme it was that had been so offensive.

I once went on *Question Time* and said that if gay marriage was OK – and I was uncertain on the issue – then I saw no reason in principle why a union should not be consecrated between three men, as well as two men; or indeed three men and a dog. Was that the remark which cheesed them off? Or was it the time when I said that among the factors responsible for the Paddington railway disaster – the fat cats, the Tories, Railtrack, etc. – you could not altogether ignore the role of the driver, who had gone through several red lights and ignored two warning buzzers in his cab? Was that what did it?

What had I done, I whimpered to myself, as I was overtaken on the running circuit by the sprightly grannies of Islington, to earn this obloquy? Why, I moaned – and did a tear mingle with the rain on my cheeks? – was I so unpopular?

And then I suppose the dopamine must have

kicked in, because I snapped out of it. Oh come off it, I said: that's what it's all about, politics. It's about being unpopular. If you dish it out, you've got to take it, you great blubbering ninny. It's a mark of honour that people should obviously hate you, as a budding politician; and if they go to the trouble to hail you in the street as a ★★★★, it is, surely, a sign that you have arrived. I scrolled back mentally through all the rebuffs and insults I had recently received, and decided to see them in a different light.

There was the taxi driver who refused to take a tip, so contorted was he with hatred for his fare. He could barely look at me as he flung the change through the window, and went off like a pin-goaded stallion, almost running over my toe.

There was the cyclist who shouted 'You tosser' and flicked me a V-sign as he overhauled me at the traffic lights. In fact, there have been several such encounters with cyclists. They seem to resent the idea that a chap like me can even be seen on a bicycle.

There was the man who shouted and threw an egg in my direction when I attended the Lawrence Inquiry at the Elephant and Castle. I am very pleased to say that I took evasive action, and that the egg splattered all over someone else. It may even have been a man from the *Guardian*.

There was the man who threatened to beat me up

in the Welsh village of Ruabon, where I was canvassing for votes in 1997. It would have been rather cool to have been beaten up, as a Tory candidate, except that my potential assailant was eighty-two and blind in one eye.

And then there are my many correspondents, who attack my parentage, my membership of the international Zionist conspiracy, the anti-Zionist conspiracy, who make disobliging personal remarks of all kinds. Well, I decided in that moment of adrenalin and dopamine: snooks to all of them. What is popularity but a sham, a snare and a delusion?

As Michael Heseltine was later to point out, in his speech in Henley town hall on the eve of the general election, the thirst for popularity is perhaps Blair's greatest vice. That, said Hezza, is why he has frittered his first term; that is why welfare is unreformed, and no real effort has been made to resolve the long-running ambiguities of Britain's relations with Europe. It is all because poor Tony wants to be loved. He craves popularity. He hungers for praise. That is why he has failed to take anything like the hard decisions which the Tories took in the early 1980s.

That, I think, was Hezza's message, and it is unquestionably right as far as it goes. Blair navigates according to the chart presented by Philip Gould and his focus groups.

Still, it must be said that the electorate are remarkably tolerant of this vice of Blair's. Popularity seems to be a useful kind of attribute if you want to win elections.

When I was selected, Matthew Parris, who was an MP in Derbyshire before becoming a seer of Fleet Street (and especially of the *Spectator*), wrote me a letter. As usual, he showed profound psychological insight. 'All Tory candidates in safe seats have a moment of panic when they think they are about to be beaten by the Liberal Democrats. Don't worry. It won't happen.'

Somehow my sang-froid is draining away today, and Parris's advice seems less and less convincing. They are everywhere, these Liberal Democrats, like self-seeding yellow poppies: kindly, principled, reasonable, and sometimes just a little bit maddening.

You can always tell the Liberals, says Chris Scott, because they refuse to say how they are going to vote. 'I'm so sorry,' they say, with an air of slight holiness, 'but that is between me and the ballot box'; or 'That is my business. I am afraid I never tell anyone how I vote, and I do not propose to start with you, young man.'

This makes it difficult to reason with them. I once spoke at a fringe meeting at a Liberal Democrat conference, on the subject of the Lib Dems and the media. It is a scandal, they said, that the media does not do more to report Lib Dem policy. You dear old things, I told them, what you don't understand is that this ignorance is the secret of your success. It's your ace card. The last thing you want is publicity for your policies, which seem at different times to include puffing ganja, raising taxes, scrapping the monarchy and doing everything Brussels tells us. No one is really sure what you stand for, except that you are somehow the nice party, the ones that refuse to indulge in the angry platitudes of the Tories and Labour. They laughed at this, acknowledging I had a point.

Such is my paranoia about the Lib Dems that I have started to develop weird superstitions. The first is the need to touch wood. As soon as I have rung the bell of a house, I try to find some wood to touch, in the hope of improving the outcome of the coming conversation. Anything will do. A quick caress of the jamb, a stroke of the sill, provided there is wood under the paint. The trouble is that some of these modern executive homes have very swish formica-type doors with nothing but white plastic integrating the frame with the brick. One householder opens up to find me leaning back gymnastically to touch the eaves of her porch. She is a Lib Dem, of course.

The other obsession I have is magpies, and the need to see two of them to avoid ill-luck. There seem to be magpies everywhere this spring. Perhaps there has been a boom in the population of dormice or voles, or whatever it is magpies eat. But they are always coming single spies, or pies. First I see one, and then another, and there is too often the nagging doubt that it may be the same bird.

Bill Deedes has a superb remedy for this neurosis. On sighting, inauspiciously, a single magpie, mutter to yourself: 'Good afternoon, Mr Magpie, and please give my regards to Mrs Magpie.' That should do the trick.

Pow! Socko! Biff!

Thursday 17 May

Appalling weather, rain slanting almost horizontally. My spirits very low. For days now the Tories have been flatlining in the polls. In fact, you could say they have been flatlining since September 1992.

I keep fantasising about what to do if I go down in history as the man who lost Henley, the first Tory to surrender the division since it was created in the mid nineteenth century. The *Telegraph* foreign desk might come up with something, for old times' sake. Bureau chief in Lagos? Stringer in Vientiane?

In this mood I take breakfast in the tea shop in Watlington, as I do most days. Anthony comes in, looking surprisingly cheerful. 'You've seen the paper,' he says.

No, I say, eating a tea-cake.

He spreads them out, incontinent with excitement.

Prescott appears to have been involved in some kind of brawl in Rhyl, not far from my former battle-ground in Clwyd South. The pictures are amazing. Here he is, the Deputy Prime Minister of the United Kingdom of Great Britain and Northern Ireland, the second most powerful (hem hem) man in the country, thumping a mullet-haired fuel protestor; and then falling backwards with him over a wall, in a great tangle of belly, jowl and fist.

'Good Lord,' I say.

'Amazing, isn't it,' says Anthony.

And there's more good news throughout the paper. Blair has been yelled at on TV. There he is, white-faced, receiving a proper tongue-lashing from some woman whose husband is a victim of the NHS. The police have heckled Straw.

I won't say we have a song on our lips, but things certainly seem to be perking up as we drive in the lashing rain to Chinnor. Could this be the turning-point of the campaign? Was this the moment when the British public, in its massive wisdom, looked more carefully at New Labour and beheld nothing but a bunch of louts and phoneys?

For some reason we are being pursued this morning by the lovely Tari Tanaka of Japanese TV, and her enormous team of sound men and cameramen. 'The sons of Nippon', as Anthony calls them, are determined to record every detail of the great British tradition of canvassing.

The people of Chinnor therefore get a shock, on opening their doors, to find not only a soaked Tory candidate, but also five shivering and beaming Japanese pointing lots of Sony gizmos at them. Heaven knows what they will make of it in Tokyo.

We have elevenses with David Wilmshurst, our county council candidate, at the Chinnor Village Centre. The implications of the Prescott punch are much discussed.

Of course it can't do them any good, we reason. How can they claim to be the party of law and order, when their Number Two is currently helping the police with their inquiries following a violent affray?

But I wonder. The more I think about it, and the more we hear the reactions from the radio phone-ins, the more it seems that Thumper Prescott will do them no harm at all; may even do them a spot of good.

What, after all, is the point of Prescott, this brooding former Cunard waiter, with his mangled syntax and his habit of inserting the definite article where it is not normally used? ('... and I tell you this, Conference, Labour will deliver the jobs and the prosperity *and* the clean environment'). He is not there to be 'Deputy Prime Minister' in any meaningful sense (that job belongs to Alastair Campbell); he is not even there to run the Department of Environment and Transport, where he has made a spectacular hash. Prescott's role is to be part of the dramaturgy of New Labour in which, by their lumpen cavortings, the Prime Minister's underlings intensify the apparent radiance of Blair. The more Prescott clowns around, the brighter Blair shines. In that respect, the punch helps.

Then to Maggie Pullen's neck of the woods for lunch, and canvassing in Berinsfield. Maggie is an astonishing figure who has been working for the Tory party and Michael Heseltine for more than a quarter of a century. She is utterly determined that we should do a full afternoon's canvassing, but the weather is indescribable. According to the paper, South Oxfordshire is the coldest place in the country. The rain won't let up, and we don't have macs or even sweaters. At one point Anthony and I find ourselves driving, hopelessly lost, down a semi-flooded road, pursued only by Hari Tanaka and the indefatigable sons of Nippon.

Anthony finds this highly amusing.

WEEK TWO

The Pace Hots Up

Educational Apartheid

Friday 18 May

'Christ on a bike,' I say to Anthony, as we have breakfast.

'I know,' he says. 'It's pretty dreadful, isn't it?'

It says here in the paper that the Tories are on 26 per cent. *The Economist* has done a poll: 26 per cent! That means we've been losing ground since the election campaign began. We try to work out how much of England will remain Tory on these figures. Perhaps just parts of Surrey, and Huntingdon, lonely blue eminences in a horrible foaming sea of red and yellow.

Actually, I don't believe it. The figure doesn't feel right. *The Economist* is simply trying to get some publicity. Perhaps it is time for the *Spectator* to commission an alternative poll.

Today the candidate receives a huge boost to his status. We go canvassing in Shiplake, home to Howard

Green, the association chairman, and guess who wants to tag along with us today? It's Jeremy Paxman!

They may have been bemused, in Chinnor and Berinsfield, to find the sons of Nippon on our tail. But to provoke the interest of Jezza Paxman, the nation's premier broadcaster: that's clout. That's kudos.

'What does Jeremy want?' asks Howard, when we gather in his sitting room. We don't really know: presumably *Newsnight* is doing an in-depth grope into the battle for Henley, the hinge of fate, the pivot of our island story.

All yesterday's meteorological wrath is abated. The sun shines, the sky is blue, the clouds fleecy, the vegetation turbo-charged with rain, and here is Paxo, on the appointed hour, in a shiny limo of some kind. But where are the film crew, the men with the furry grey candyfloss? It's just Paxo, looking distinctly off-duty, in jeans and a pair of oxblood leather shoes. He seems to be carrying a small notebook, presumably made by Smythson or Turnbull and Asser.

It appears he is here researching a book. We all experience the mixture of disappointment and relief that comes when you find you are not, after all, likely to appear on television. 'Lead on,' says Jethro Paxman. 'Just pretend I'm not here.'

Nor is anyone else, as it turns out. Shiplake is sunk in quiet, and it is some time before we can produce a voter for the great man to inspect.

Here is a couple carrying the freshly creosoted A-frame of a new summerhouse. Hello, I say, and am introducing myself when the chap says, yes, he knows exactly who I am, and he won't shake hands because they are covered with creosote, but he may as well tell me he doesn't think much of me.

In fact, he says, he thinks I am a very far from adequate successor to Michael Heseltine. Not to put too fine a point on it, he says, he thinks I am a bit of a clown. This rather gets in amongst me, since it is by far the most hostile reception I have encountered in almost ten months of campaigning.

I am sorry to have given that impression, I say. What were you thinking of in particular? A certain iciness may have crept into my tone. It seems he thought something I said on the radio was flippant. Just as I am preparing to try to put him straight, my mobile phone rings.

Of course, I should have turned the thing off. Not only is it rude to let your mobile interrupt a conversation you have yourself initiated; there is nothing more important than a voter. But I find myself stalking off, and indignantly telling whoever has rung that I am talking to a man who thinks I am a clown.

All in all, a fairly catastrophic piece of campaigning.

Rule number one: the customer is always right.

Thankfully Jeremy Paxman misses this exchange. He is dawdling at the back, and does not seem to be following the Johnson Story with complete attention. The thesis of his book, it turns out, is that politics and politicians don't really matter much these days. Politicians, Paxo will argue in his new book, are not worth a pitcher of warm spit, especially not compared with multinational tycoons and the Olympian journalist figures who nightly mould the mind of the country with their cross-examinations, at once brutal and Socratic. That makes my career decision odd, in Paxman's view.

'Why are you going into it, Boris?' says Jeremy, as we trudge around the lovely leafy lanes of Shiplake.

My first observation to Paxman is that his idea – that politics is limited in its impact – has a long ancestry. 'How small, of all that human hearts endure,' said Oliver Goldsmith, 'That part which laws or kings can cause or cure!'

In so far as that is true, it is a good thing. And yet politicians still pre-empt about 40 per cent of our national wealth, and spend it on our behalf. What they do is not trivial; and you could argue that, on that measurement alone, they are more important than ever.

As for me, why am I doing it, Jeremy? I tell him:

it's 30 per cent a desire to be of public service or use, or however you want to express that with minimal piety. It is 40 per cent sheer egomania; and it is 30 per cent attributable to the belief that the world ought not to be run by swankpot journalists, showing off and kicking politicians around, when they haven't tried to do any better themselves, hmm, what, hmmm?

Paxo snorts cheerfully and pretends to write this down. He thinks I am being satirical, but I am not entirely – at least not in the point about service. You notice that a lot of journalists, when they find themselves nel mezzo del cammin di nostra vita, start to be afflicted by Doubts. Is it Enough, they ask themselves, just to file my stuff, tootle off to the pub and then stagger home? Should I not be Putting Something Back In?

I have noticed some of my friends suddenly saying, Right, that's it, I'm off to work for Oxfam in the Sudan; or I'm going to found the British wing of Médecins Sans Frontières. It would be trying the reader's credulity to say that one goes into politics for exactly the same reasons that one decides to help the starving in Africa. But I don't think the two sets of motivations are always a million miles apart. Who knows what Paxo will do next, once he has had his fill of beating up politicians?

At lunch he reveals that he is in favour of the death

penalty. That's right. Paxo's a bit of a hanger, if not a flogger. Not a lot of people know that.

As we part I ask him how much he's got out of us for his book, after spending the better part of a day on our case. 'Oh,' he says gloomily, 'about two hundred words.'

Saturday 19 May

You wouldn't guess it, to look at this crowd, but some of them have been very naughty during the night. They got up in their dormies and, perhaps fortified by sloe gin and other bits of a midnight feast, they stole out into the Quadrangle. Then they opened a tin of pink paint and desecrated the ancient cannon that symbolises the martial valour of the school's alumni. Then they painted pink footprints all over the place. Ever since the outrage was reported, at first light, the headmaster, Clive Dytor, has debated how to administer retribution.

Now in my day, of course, we would have been given at least six whacks of the cane. These, though, are more merciful times; and even if the custom had not been outlawed by the European Convention on Human Rights, Clive doesn't really want to begin the school's Speech Day with a vast thrashing of the senior boys.

So they goggle back at me with a pretence of politeness, and you cannot tell who are the good boys and who are the miscreants. They all have blazers tidy, hair slicked, spots more or less under control. When I come to speak, they laugh at my sallies. Their parents sit among them, all of them also looking very smart in pearls or tweeds or both.

If sometimes I see an eyelid stealing slowly downwards, that is no comment on their manners, since the atmosphere in the hall is stifling. But first, Clive stands before them, in a long black MA gown, and behind him are ranged the other teachers, also looking pretty scholastic. To the right of the lectern, where Clive is speaking, there are piled shiny new books, interleaved with pieces of paper to show the name of the boy who has won them. Clive is tall, with dark hair, a Cambridge graduate who fought in the Falklands. He generally exudes Arnoldian firmness and pedagogical courage.

His remarks would be thought hysterically unfashionable these days, all about the virtues of Cardinal Newman, who founded this school. All in, the scene is an advertisement for the benefits of a public school education. As Clive speaks on, I allow my mind to wander over the dilemmas of our system.

There are many good schools in South Oxfordshire, fee-paying and state schools alike. I have spoken to many of them. At one school I received a cheer for my end of term speech, in what the headmaster later told me was an unprecedented accolade. This was partly because they liked my speech on the subject of 'failure' (a great British talent, ladies and gentlemen and boys and girls: I give you Captain Scott, Eddie the Eagle Edwards, the Tory party). But mainly they liked it because it turned into a quiz on Harry Potter, where they all seemed to know all the answers – a central principle of modern education.

I have also spoken to audiences in the big comprehensives; and sometimes I went down well, and sometimes I had a bit of a grilling. All the schools had their good points; but one truth is inescapable.

The children in the state schools simply do not have the advantages – in facilities, in teacher time, in sports, languages, ballet, drama, fretwork and the chance to build their own car – that are given to the children in the private, fee-paying schools. Go to the state schools, and you will see many good things: bright children, hard work, dedicated teachers and all the rest of it. But you will also see classrooms in peeling portakabins, with condensation running down the walls, and far too many to a room. You will find children slouching past teachers with their hands in their pockets (I know it sounds weird to complain, but it just wasn't allowed at my school). There are crisp packets blowing about, and the teachers have the strain on their faces of trying to deal with too many pupils and too little cash.

If you talk to the officials of Oxfordshire County Council, you find they believe that there is a link, alas, between private sector success, and public sector difficulty. The number and quality of private schools in the county has an effect, inevitably, on the state schools. They cream off the middle-class kids who can afford it. The result is the perpetuation of Britain's educational apartheid.

They think we are crazy, in France and Germany, to bleed ourselves white, out of taxed income, to send our children to fee-paying schools. But the middle classes, especially in the inner cities, feel they have no choice. If they live in, say, Islington, they find the quality of secondary school education seems to be roughly on a par with Burkina Faso (some Botswanan teachers came on an exchange, and were horrified at what they saw). So they pull them out at eleven, or before, and put them into the private system, or, like Tony and Cherie, they find a very good state school miles away at the other end of London.

Either way, the apartheid marches on. What to do? You could abolish the public schools, but that would be odious. No political leader, not even the Old Fettesian Tony Blair, would contemplate that. So you are left with the task of improving the state schools, and if there is one reason for admiring Blair it is that he has pushed education up the agenda. His ideas may seem vague, and his bluster about private sector solutions unconvincing. But at least he talks about it, and seems to realise how colossally important it is. That is more than could be said for some of the Tories, during their long reign.

My own thoughts on state education are heavily influenced by our experience in London. We have seen how a struggling primary school, in a pretty unpromising area, can be transformed by the efforts and imagination of one man. Within five years of his arrival he had visibly galvanised the teachers and moved the school to the top of the league table in Islington, which may not be saying much, but it is saying something. He has an earring, which my Tory audiences sometimes find comical. He has proved to be a first-rate headmaster.

So I tend to bang on about the importance of letting good teachers get on with it, and liberating them from local authority control, and that kind of thing. But as I grasp the lectern now, at the school in Goring, I have another idea. By good fortune, I have just discovered my notes of this oration. This is what I say:

'It is a great honour to be asked to speak at your prize-giving, but also rather terrifying, because in the canon of English literature these occasions are normally marked by some disaster. There is the moment when Gussie Fink-Nottle gives out the prizes at Market Snodsbury Grammar School, and decides that P. K. Purvis had cheated in order to win the prize for scripture knowledge. This provoked a revolt among the parents.

'The only other time I have been called on to do this was at my former prep school, and then my trouser fly burst in a conspicuous way just before I was due to go on, and had to be repaired publicly by the headmaster's wife.

'But any terror I might feel was magnified as I came up the drive, because I have been here before, ladies and gentlemen, as a nervous adolescent. I have come here before, knees trembling, heart knocking against my ribs, because we used to play this school at rugby, and I remember the encounters as raw, unprincipled and heavy with the thud of bone on bone.

'I cannot now remember who won – blessed amnesia has descended – but I have a memory of children sobbing softly as they were ground into the mud, and hands turning mottled orange and blue in the sleet, and the chilblains and the awful smell of Deep Heat. And of course it made me what I am.

'Whatever you may think of team games, however much you may abominate them, and yearn to get on with something more entertaining behind the bike shed, you must accept that they have something to do with the success of great schools like this one, which are admired not just in this country, but across Europe.

'And I think of rugby now, because, as some of you may know, I have been wandering around this area a great deal, recently, in search of votes. Now I am under strict instructions from Clive not to make a party political broadcast. It is my intention that this speech should not contain a word of politics. Any babies here are at no risk of being kissed, at least by me.

'But I do want to relay the words of one man I met in Chinnor, who asked me what I could do about the teenage tearaways, the fifteen- and sixteen-year-olds who loafed around in the evenings with nothing to do. They bared their bottoms at the newsagent, he said. Other shopkeepers have told me that they spit at the windows and run away: which may sound trivial, but which, in the end, can get you down. "If you can solve that, and find something for these kids to do, then you will get my vote," he said.

'And I fell to thinking what I had in my education, and which other children did not have; and of course these are likely to be the things that you have, in your education, which other children do not have.

'And now I am going to sound immensely crusty and fogeyish, for a thirty-six-year-old, but I believe that one thing we have lost in our educational system is respect. When I was at school, pathetic though it may sound, we were full of respect for our teachers. We called them sir. They were people of authority, who not only instructed us, but communicated a vague sense of awe.

'Well, I have children in state primary education, and I have to tell you that times have changed. They call teachers by their first names, which was not the case when I was in state primary education. The teachers have no power whatsoever to discipline them, terrified as they are of the great engine of state retribution if they are felt in any way to have infringed the rights of the child.

'And so I felt that part of the answer might be to do ...'

You may or may not be relieved to know that my notes cut off at this point. The rest of the speech has been lost to history, along with respect for teachers. Broadly speaking, I said that there are many ways you might try restoring this dignity to the profession.

You could give them more money. More productively – and thinking of the success of Steve, our earringed head teacher – you could stop treating them as mere utensils of the Whitehall bureaucrat, mechanically churning through the same identical and excessive paperwork. You could restore their authority in the classroom in one small way. If they are involved in a disciplinary incident that would have been commonplace twenty years ago – slapping a child for dangerous behaviour, say – then you don't parade their names in the press until the affair has been cleared up. All that might be popular with teachers. In return, they would have to earn respect, of course, in their results. That is always slightly less popular.

Pompous though they sound, I was rather proud of my thoughts on respect. I genuinely believe they offer a theme, if not a programme, for action. Marina, to my chagrin, thinks it is all a bit thin.

And when I am canvassing a couple of days later, and find a woman clipping her yew, she tells me with a smirk that she much enjoyed my speech at her son's school. 'Mind you,' she says, 'I thought you were a bit bonkers. You seemed to be saying that rugby was the answer to the problems of state education.'

To which I respond stiffly that she cannot really have been listening.

No, ma'am, I say. Not rugby. Respect.

'Respect,' I say, and make a special Ali G sign.

Another Tense Moment

You know, I have this funny feeling there is a gender difference in operation here. We are canvassing in Thame, and as you hail a couple with a pram, you notice that very often the man says, yeah, fine, thumbs up, I'm with you all the way, and the woman doesn't say anything.

Hang on a mo, you say to the woman, what about you? And she gives a sort of Mona Lisa smile and says she's still making her mind up.

Now what is going on? Is it that the women are just less embarrassed about admitting that they haven't decided? Or is it possible – help – that we Tories are just a little bit more of a turn-off to women? I'll say one thing for Blair: he's got the family man thing locked up.

Just think how utterly magnificent it would be if the word were to go out from Central Office that

Ffion was with child. If I were Italian I might go down to the local church and do one of those ex-voto offerings of a pewter baby.

Talking of religious experiences, the Lord might as well let his servant depart in peace, for I have seen my salvation. Have just been canvassing with Diana Ludlow, our northern-born candidate for Thame. She is a hugely vigorous woman with ringleted hair, who has survived a bad car crash. She was on life support at Stoke Mandeville for months; she wasn't meant to live. Now you only have to sit with her in her adapted car, or watch her walk, to sense the strength of her will.

We pitch up at a big block of sheltered accommodation. Diana and I are doing alternate doors, thrusting our literature into the uncomplaining hands of the old folk. Then we come across one of those rare cases where there is something you, as a politician, might actually do to help. There is a man whose wheelchair is so unwieldy, or perhaps the doorway is so tight, that his wife can't even get him to the lift down the hall. The result is that she can't take him out, and she hardly gets out herself.

'They said we could have a downstairs flat,' she moans, and it seems that the authorities keep breaking their promise. Her daughter from the West Country has arrived to help, and the two of them – both sizeable women – are overwrought with anger. Is there anything I can do to help? they ask. I really wish I could, I mumble, feeling genuinely sorry for them. The man can be heard making noises off, groaning from down the corridor and asking, 'Who is it?'

And then Diana arrives, and she asks what the problem is. They pour it out, and soon both women have tears running down their cheeks, as they show us the letter of complaint they have drawn up – massive, hand-written – and begin to shake with sobs. By this stage I have retreated behind Diana, feeling oppressed by my impotence and the extent of their suffering.

Suddenly Diana says, 'Now just hush a minute, and hold your hands out'; and, blinking, they both do as they are told. Then she lays her hands on theirs, and their crying subsides. There is a long silence, and they stand there with heads bowed.

At this point I must confess that owing to some defect in my character I have to bite the inside of my cheek very hard. But at the end of it the women seem markedly more cheerful; Diana takes a note of their problem, and seems to think she can sort it out.

Now that is brilliant, I think to myself, as we leave. If I could do that kind of thing, I'd have it made.

We're at a jumble sale in Wheatley, and we are all milling around, trying to mingle and look amiable. One of the trestles bears a big, solid-looking cricket bat, and I give it a trial swipe. I am a fundamentally useless cricketer, but when my mind is in repose (i.e. quite often) I find myself performing imaginary drives, hooks and Bothamesque thuds over the bowler's head.

My reverie is interrupted by the sight of a man in a green sweater, walking around the stalls saying, 'Vote for me, vote for me,' in a manner which seems to be ever so slightly satirical. I try to introduce myself, in the hope of making him desist.

After a while we all file out, having bought and eaten quite a few cupcakes and drunk quite a bit of tea. We have not, however, bought any of the actual merchandise. There follows a moment of surpassing dreadfulness.

We are standing outside the Merry Bells hall – Glenys, self, Anthony and others – saying hello to the passers-by, when I become aware of a young girl tugging my sleeve.

Her face is red, whether from embarrassment or anger I am not sure. She is trembling, and as she speaks it suddenly occurs to me that she has been rehearsing these words, and that she is only about fifteen or sixteen. 'Why haven't you done anything to support the local community?' she says.

I look at her blankly. Glenys interrupts: 'But we have. We've bought plenty of coffee,' she says.

'You say you've bought plenty of coffee,' says the

girl, 'but you haven't done anything to support the local community. You haven't bought any jumble,' she says to me, ramming the point home.

I feel terrible. She's quite right: ghastly, self-satisfied politicians going round a village hall, beaming, glad-handing, schmoozing, and they can't even be bothered to dip into their own pockets in support of the cause concerned.

I rush back into the hall and look for something to buy. Perhaps it is my paranoia, but I feel everyone has been talking about us, discussing our rudeness and stinginess. Aha, I think, and grab the cricket bat. 'How much is it?' I ask the man.

'That's twenty-five p,' he says.

'Here you are,' I say, and give him a pound.

'You can't buy my vote,' says the man.

By this point my nerves are so stretched that I put the coin firmly into his palm and say, quite loudly: 'I'm not trying to buy your vote. I'm trying to buy a cricket bat. You can vote for whoever you like.'

About twenty minutes later, after Anthony and I have been driving in total silence to our next destination, I say: 'That was awful. I shouldn't have snapped like that.'

Anthony pauses and says, 'You did snap. It was the first time I have heard you do that.'

The Viagra Effect

Sunday 20 May

Oh Lord, oh Lord, the polls, the polls. The polls aren't getting any better at all. According to the *Sunday Telegraph*, there is some sort of schism at the top of the party. Some say we spent too long shoring up our core vote, talking about Europe, asylum-seekers, law and order, etc., when we should have been addressing the 'issues which really matter' to 'real people' in the 'real world'.

In other words, we should have campaigned much more vociferously on health, education and other areas of government failure. Yeah, well: it's possible, it's possible. You certainly get a lot about health and education on the doorstep. But what do I know?

Fighting an election is like being sent upriver, into the heart of the jungle. All my lines of communication with the metropolis are down. The TV at Swyncombe only seems to get Channel 4, and that's pretty fuzzy. I have no radio, and sometimes go for days without properly reading the paper.

No one comes to see us from Central Office, and though we receive excellent briefings on the issues of the day, and the campaign themes, it all seems rather remote.

Maybe they'll find me still fighting, months after the Tories have experienced another Hiroshima, like those Japanese soldiers in the Spratly Islands or wherever it was.

So what do you want me to do for you? I ask, Uriah Heep-like, on the doorstep. Tell me what the issues are that matter to you. 'I tell you one thing,' says one magnificent woman in her forties, folding her arms in front of her. 'I couldn't give a monkey's about health and education.' I want to hug her.

It does wonders for the old one-eyed trouser snake, says my friend the Oxfordshire GP, motioning with her hand to show the effects of the pill. One minute it's like that – her slim arm hangs limply; and the next minute, *pow*. My canvassing team and I look at the angle of inclination of her arm, which is now about forty-five degrees. We are impressed. But even more extraordinary than the physiological effects of Viagra, says the GP – let us call her Laura – is the way it dissolves the male sense of inhibition.

In the old days, she says, people from the village could barely spit it out when they came to discuss their penile non-turgor factor. 'They used to shuffle their feet and look at the floor, and sort of kick the radiator, and then say that they had this friend who had a problem. And now,' says Laura, 'you wouldn't believe how they behave. They march into the surgery, take out a load of twenty-pound notes, slap them on the counter and sing out, Morning, Moneypenny (or whatever the name of the practice's secretary is), I'll have fifteen Viagra, please. Or they say, Morning, dearie, have you got my Viagra ready?' As though they were buying half a pound of plums or a pack of shotgun shells. She has prescribed twenty-four Viagra treatments in the last two years. The interesting thing, she says, is how the focus of male embarrassment has shifted. If impotence is merely a physical thing that can be sorted out with a wonderful blue lozenge, then it is no longer a matter for shame. Taking Viagra nowadays is no more exceptional, to her patients, than taking aspirin to thin the blood.

Isn't that fascinating? I say. Presumably the potential cause of embarrassment has shifted upwards and backwards to the mind, the centre of the sexual urge. In these days of mandatory sexual activity, the real disgrace would be a weakness of the spirit, not the flesh.

Nowadays, one imagines, the embarrassing thing would be not even to want to buy the Viagra in the first place.

Hmm, says Laura; all she could say about the men of South Oxfordshire is that they are a pretty virile bunch. Consider the great and growing cohort of men in their sixties, seventies, eighties and – who knows? – nineties. They are fitter, healthier and richer than ever before. They have time on their hands, and they want loads of Viagra. In fact, she says, laughing, it is the women who are starting to complain. 'I've had some wives begging me to stop prescribing it so much. You know, there they are, thinking they are going to have a quiet night, and they get the old rod in the back, if you don't mind the expression.'

Not at all, I say, and just remind me, how much is this Viagra, per pill? She tells me that it is £8 per shot, and that it has a funny effect on the cones of your retina, so that you see blue at the critical moment.

My only purpose in asking is ideological: to see how readily people will pay for something in a doctor's surgery, if they really want it, and if the state won't cough up. Think of all these priapic males in South Oxfordshire, happily investing in the magic pill and making the nights hell for their wives. A simple cash transaction, between health service and consumer, producing instant satisfaction. And then consider all those other health services which are funded by the state, and which are rationed by delay and by availability: the trolley waits for hip transplants, the brutal last-minute angioplasty cancellations, the day you came to have your cataracts done, and there weren't enough nurses. Aha, I think: terrific. Viagra could become a fresh text for my sermon about the beauties of putting private money into the NHS, a point already adumbrated in the parable of the toast (see above).

I remember how one hot evening I was talking to Thame Rotary Club, and I challenged them: should rhinoplasty be free at the point of delivery to anyone who wants it? Should liposuction? Should gender reassignment? And what about Viagra, ladies and gentlemen? No one seemed to think that any of these things should be free. Whenever I speak about the NHS at public meetings, and before exclusively Tory audiences, everyone seems, on the face of it, to agree with me that the system is in need of reform. They know it isn't working. They can see that the government's tinkering with waiting lists is producing a load of abstract 'triumphs', rather like Stalinist figures for sorghum yields in Siberia. According to my friend Dr Laura, the waiting list gerrymandering is actually pernicious, diverting doctors from urgent to non-urgent cases in order to accomplish some Whitehall-dictated quota.

Time and again I make these points in my

speeches on health. Yes, they spend more per capita on health care in France, Germany, Belgium and just about every comparable European country. And yes, it is true that this produces results. If you are diagnosed with stomach cancer, you have a 5 per cent chance of surviving five years in the United Kingdom, a 24 per cent chance in France, and a 35 per cent chance in Germany. No wonder so many UK patients want to take advantage of one of their few positive benefits as EU 'citizens', and travel overseas for operations. But it is also true, if you look at these other European countries, that they have a far larger private health-care sector; and you have to ask yourself, as we prepare to spend more of our national wealth on health, how it should be done.

You can continue to believe in the NHS as the sole and sufficient provider; and you can continue to pump the money all the way through the Whitehall tubing, leaking like some enormous Saharan water-pipe, and hope that it ends up providing the service you want. Or you can conclude that this is one of the reasons why we have a system which treats the patients as dolts and serfs, pushing them from hospital to hospital and keeping them waiting on trolleys. You may think it quite right that the common-law wife of a patient can shout at Tony Blair, on television, because he is the de facto head of her health service. Or you might reflect that in most other European countries it would seem bizarre so to blame the Prime Minister, and that Britain is the last home of socialist medicine.

My point is not that we should scrap the NHS; of course not. But in so far as we push new money into health, we should shorten the distance that money travels between leaving our pockets – as taxpayers or premium-payers – and buying the operation or service we need. As it happens, Dr Laura, my friend the South Oxfordshire GP, is more robust. 'Privatise the lot,' she tells me.

And usually, as I say, these points – once taboo – are increasingly well taken, especially during this election. Such is people's dissatisfaction with Labour, and its failure to keep its promises on health, that they are genuinely willing to consider alternatives. I only ran into trouble twice. The first time it was just some small arms fire, nothing serious. One man put his hand up after a speech in Watlington, and put his finger on the problem. Look here, he said: you say you want to have more private spending on health. But isn't that just another tax, in a different form? I had to admit that he was quite right. On the other hand, whether the money was spent as tax or insurance, it was always our money. The more we had control of it, I suggested, the more chance we had of holding to account those who were spending it on our behalf; and the more chance we had of securing whatever treatment it was we needed. He seemed more or less satisfied with this, though with some harrumphing.

The second time was at a speech to the Windsor Medical Society, and here the flak was so heavy that I almost came down in flames. It was an after-dinner job in some hotel by the castle, and I'd given a jolly-ish speech in which I'd made, I think, the point about the toast. Suddenly I became aware of rumblings and groanings on my right. One of the tables seemed to be conspicuously more left-wing than the others, and a man with a beard was ranting at me.

'You just want to privatise the NHS!'

'No I don't,' I said.

'Yes, you do,' he said.

'No, I don't,' I said, and soon a great counter-barracking was going on from other tables, as the man with the beard continued to rave about years of underfunding, and so on.

The trick of after-dinner speeches is to keep them light. But this one was a goner. My undercarriage was hopelessly snarled in the jungle, and it was necessary, pretty soon, to make a forced landing. My only consolation was that afterwards one of the doctors, an Asian, came up and said he agreed with every word. Oh, and I also got a not inconsiderable honorarium from the Windsor Medical Society for making the speech.

They're not all poor, these doctors.

There is a pretty large measure of agreement about the way to improve health care in this country. Whichever party finally buckles to, the task will not be easy. The Tories will struggle to overcome the suspicion of the NHS-worshipping public and the public sector professionals. Labour will struggle to overcome the deep ideological reservations of their key supporters. If they had their way, of course, Viagra would be 'free'; except that it would be rationed by postcode, or delay, and by the time the state actually coughed up your little blue pill you might find that your libido had vanished. Which might, or might not, be a matter of some relief to your wife.

I meet an elderly couple in Wheatley who raise the issue of bus tokens. They are deeply exercised by the problem, and it tumbles from their lips in all its intricacy. In fact, I have to ask them to repeat it several times. It seems that you can choose to have a half-price bus pass, or tokens to the value of £20. Some parishes subsidise the tokens, but not Wheatley. 'We feel like second-class citizens,' say the old couple. What am I going to do about it?

You might as well ask me to solve the Schleswig-Holstein question, I think; but am immediately overcome by irritation with my own laziness. Here I am, presuming to offer myself as their MP.

These people are living in South Oxfordshire, a vast area served by private, deregulated bus companies. They may have no car. Or they may be unable to pay the crippling price of petrol, thanks to Gordon Brown's excise duties (Tory hear-hears). Someone in my position should damn well understand the difficulties of his putative constituents in moving from A to B.

So I conduct some research. I assemble huge quantities of bumf, and I try to work it out. Suppose I am a little old lady living in a small South Oxfordshire village, and my husband is in intensive care, having been bitten by a crazed South African-owned dog. Am I better off having a bus pass or tokens, if I want to visit him in the John Radcliffe?

After some hours coddling my brain, it strikes me that bus tokens are handy if my journey additionally involves a taxi or a train, since they are also accepted on taxis and trains. But they don't go very far. You only receive £20 worth of bus tokens per year.

In other words, much depends on how badly my husband has been bitten. If he has a serious wound, in the testicles, for instance, then I might need to visit him many times before he is well. In those circumstances, it might be better to have a bus pass. On the other hand, there are some routes where bus passes are not accepted at all.

Oh dear. What can I do about it, eh? As I stare from my Swyncombe window, I seem to see a limitless vista of human inconvenience and botheration. I see a great mountain of transport problems, and I wonder how I can lift a pebble from it, without simply using more taxpayers' money?

What can I, a mere Tory candidate, a mere toenail, hope to accomplish, if the solution has eluded the minds of South Oxfordshire District Council?

On the other hand, you never know. I might come up with something.

A Pig Farmer's Story

Monday 21 May

Orpwood the farmer breathes heavily, and his moustache quivers like an exhaling walrus. 'It's a nightmare,' he says, leaning on his stave. Now Orpwood, or Orpie, as he is known, is not a man given to gloom. He is a large, bounding sort of optimist.

There have been early mornings when I am lying in bed and pondering my campaign strategy when I hear a buzz, and it is Orpie on his quad bike, come to chivvy me out for a cup of coffee. Over the months I have had several fine meals with my neighbours, produced from the Aga by his wife Jean. Her speciality is roast suckling pig, lovingly reared on the farm. And as you pile on the apple sauce, and debate which is crisper, the crackling or the potatoes, you experience sensations of enthusiasm for the farming life.

Imagine it: living here, high on the Chilterns. You

rise to see the dawn as it flatters your green meadows with a sovereign eye. You spend the morning lambing or farrowing, or on some other socially useful task. You have lunch with your chums in the Crown in Pishill. You go shooting whenever you want. If you are lucky, you have roast pork for supper, with its gunfire crackling. And every day you are out in the open, looking out for many miles over the plain of South Oxfordshire below. There is nothing between you and the Wittenham Clumps, which were painted by Constable, and the cooling towers of Didcot, which were not. There is nothing above you but the blue spring sky, and the wheeling red kites they have recently reintroduced.

Yes, you think, in your naïve, citified way, there is much to be said for the Orpwood existence: until your friend the farmer sighs again, and explains the problem. It is not that he has been up in the lambing byre since three, though that may be true. 'It's the uncertainty,' he says. That's what's getting him down, and many other farmers like him.

He has 500 pigs, and they are all ready to go off for the next stage of their careers. It may be slaughter; it may be more fattening – I can't work it out – but he needs them out of here, soon, and MAFF says he can't move them. Like other farmers in South Oxfordshire, David and Jean Orpwood have not experienced foot and mouth directly, touch wood, but the knock-on effects are everywhere. Like the rest of rural Britain, they have the disinfectant-soaked straw at the farm entrance. And they have their stock under total Whitehall control. The men from MAFF may not know what they are doing; they may decide one thing this week and another thing the next; but they are in charge. The risk is growing of a financial disaster, of a kind farmers are experiencing throughout the country.

As you walk round the farm with Jean, you have a sense of how tough it can be; how easily your commercial expectations can be messed up. There has been much rain this spring (an understatement). You would have thought this was good news. To judge by the hawthorn, and its exuberant nuptial whiteness, you would have thought the meadows were in good shape. But no. For some reason the grass doesn't like too much rain. The ewes aren't making enough milk. There seem to be about twenty underfed lambs. They must be bottle-fed, and in this my children try to assist.

Now, I've bottle-fed lambs. As I did not hesitate to point out during the selection procedure, I have rural roots. My grandmother used to keep the weakest lambs in the bottom oven of the Aga, just like Jean Orpwood. I remember how tricky they can be to bottle-feed – the way they tug the teat in the wrong direction, and the milk spurts over their lips. But then we Johnsons eventually gave up, sold our stock, and our family farm's best ever financial performance was a £50 loss. The Orpwoods are still at it, and when a sheep dies, as sheep do, that's money. My children are fascinated by the sight of a dead lamb, and give small sentimental cries. For Jean Orpwood, I expect, a dead lamb is just another minor dent in the wallet.

The Orpwoods will be all right. Orpie is head of the Oxfordshire NFU, and runs a big, efficient farm. Other farmers are very far from all right.

When you talk to farmers, you often have the sense that they see themselves as victims of inscrutable cosmic forces. They are as flies to wanton boys, and among the implacable divinities there is MAFF, which tells them whether and when they may move their pigs. There is the Brussels commission, with its strange pipe-puffing Frenchmen in oatmeal-coloured offices, who decide the price at which they may export their wheat, and what premium they receive for a ewe. There are planners and environmentalists and food freaks who heap regulations on them, who slaughter the local abattoirs and raise their costs. There is Gordon Brown, who so extravagantly taxes the petrol in their 4x4s. And then there are the supermarkets, who, more than anyone else, seem to wield the knout over the yeoman farmers of England.

For the last three years farm incomes have been

falling. Farming has been in crisis, and at times the entire countryside feels as though it is in crisis. Pubs close, shops close, as the population metamorphoses into a commuter population and villages become a gaggle of second homes. I must have visited eight South Oxfordshire shop-cum-post offices during the course of the campaign, and found four that were on the point of closing down, rate relief or no rate relief. Don't underestimate that point about the village shop. You may suspect that it's sentimental twaddle to say that it gives a focus to a community and that the old dears need it for the pension-book gossip. But it's true, and it's certainly felt in the villages. And to cap it all, the Labour townees want to ban hunting. I can't tell you how much it means to some country people. I don't just mean the posh folk. I mean the farmers with broad Oxfordshire accents, for whom hunting is a relief from the weekly grind, something to look forward to, a chance for a get-together in a notoriously lonely profession.

They come to meetings, and they listen patiently to my babble about Europe, and health, and public services, and then they come up to me afterwards, in their woollen ties and their check shirts, and say quietly, 'You'll be all right on hunting, won't you?' Oh yes, I say, don't worry. I am a sympathiser. 'But are you a supporter?' they say quickly, detecting a wishy-washy word. Yes, I say. I will never vote to ban hunting. It is a piece of spite that has nothing to do with animal welfare, and everything to do with Blair's manipulation of rank-and-file Labour chippiness and class hatred. Like most farmers round here, Orpwood has been on the Countryside March. Had the last one not been cancelled because of foot and mouth, you would have seen him on your TV, leading a group in T-shirts designed by Michael Heath with the slogan BLAIR DOESN'T CARE. That is a message that he and his kind have been successful in putting across.

You can see it in the pages of the *Daily Telegraph*, not just the rage of the shires, but the rage of the suburbs for the insult done to the shires. You can see it in the bumper stickers on the backs of the Volvos and Land Rover Discoveries in Fulham. In the imagination of rural Britain, Blair is a metropolitan flippertigibbet who knows and cares nothing about their pains. His ministers would rather be chowing down in some Conran super-brasserie than finding out the troubles of those who actually put the food on the table. They don't want to risk getting mud on their trouser-legs, the nancy-boys. That is how the government is seen by large chunks of rural Britain. The question is, what the government can reasonably be expected to do.

Take supermarkets. In a hotly contested field, it is the supermarkets which arouse the British middle classes to their greatest fever of hypocrisy. We know how nasty they are to the farmers, acting as sole buyers and setting such miserly prices that they drive their suppliers into the red. We know how they turn down good British apples, which may have the odd wart, in favour of smooth-skinned products from France. We know how the supermarket tycoons suck up to the Labour government, and vice versa: how Lord Sainsbury is a minister of science, and responsible for genetically modified crops. There is Tesco, which gave Blair £12 million towards the Millennium Dome, and was rewarded shortly thereafter when Labour dropped its plan for a tax on supermarket car parks. We have read that supermarkets drive such a hard bargain with the sheep farmers of Exmoor that they are driven to shoot their flocks rather than trying to sell them; and sometimes shoot themselves.

We may even think it a shame that planning permission has been given so liberally for out-of-town superstores. We pretend that we miss the old days, when you waited in the sawdust-strewn grocer's, your car on a meter, while a man in a white coat stood on a stepladder and reached you down a tin of beans or Fray Bentos steak and kidney pie. But when the children are bawling, and we need to knock off the weekly shop in an hour and a half, and we want fresh mangetout flown in from Kenya – boy, do we love our supermarkets. To rail against Sainsbury's, or Waitrose, as is sometimes fashionable, is really humbug.

As for 'reforming the Common Agricultural Policy', which has been promised by every British government in memory, it's not happening. There have been two reforms in the last ten years, both allegedly far-reaching and fundamental, but the essence of the system remains unchanged.

We have been moving away from the export refund system, which encourages the EU to dump its produce on the world market. Slowly, under pressure from the Americans and from the former Commonwealth countries, we are chipping away at the system of market support, by which the taxpayer is stung twice, once in propping up the price, and once in paying for the food. In an ideal world, subsidy would be targeted at the incomes of farmers who need it, and not the barley barons of East Anglia. But progress is glacial.

Then there is deregulation, one of the most wretched subjects in British politics. Whatever they say, ministers just don't believe in it, not when they might be the ones who are held responsible for the relaxation of the rules which led to BSE, or salmonella in egg production.

Is there any hope? At the risk of infuriating Orpwood and others, it is always worth pointing out that the industry has biblical cycles, lean years and fat years. Farmers had seven good years, and they have just had four bad years. Ultimately the best thing for farmers might be to lose, gradually, their sense that they are the victims of a cold, unfeeling fate. In Orpwood's view, at least, they need to take more charge of their own lives, and assert their independence as economic actors, raising high-value, premium stuff and, if possible, marketing it themselves.

To see one way of doing this, get on down to the farmers' markets that have sprung up in Henley, Thame and elsewhere over the last few years. There you will find people selling sausages they have made themselves, and lavender honey they have harvested, and even a kind of English Parmesan cheese. You will also find David and Jean Orpwood selling lamb and pork, complete with instructions about how to reproduce that crackling effect. 'It's amazing we can do this at this price,' Orpie will tell you as he sells you a joint of pork.

You may agree, when you look at the label, that the price is certainly amazing. But I assure you that when you get home, and shove it in the oven, you will have value for money, and to judge by the number of joints he sells, I am not alone in that view.

More Gaffes and Goofs

Tuesday 22 May

To Oxford West and Abingdon, an adjoining seat, to offer fraternal support in the form of joint canvassing. This is a seat we can win and must win if we are to have any hope of forming a government. The incumbent is Dr Evan Harris, a spaniel-eyed Lib Dem who was at Oxford with me. The rampaging Tory challenger is Ed Matts, who was also at Oxford with me. No shortage of Oxford men in these Oxfordshire seats, eh.

For four glorious years I was the tight-head prop of the Balliol XV, while Matts was the loose-head prop of the Christ Church XV. He claims to remember playing against me. In fact, he says, he 'stuffed me up all afternoon'. I have no recollection of this.

The boast seems plausible, however, when I consider Matts's SAS-style canvassing techniques. We are standing in the sun outside some school, running the gauntlet of the mums, many of them looking very pretty in their summer dresses. I am doing the Uriah Heep 'Hello, sorry to trouble you but I wonder whether I can possibly introduce myself ...' routine, and mainly getting the brush-off.

Matts, on the other hand, is confidence itself, like the kid at the school disco who already knows about girls. 'Ed Matts,' he booms, thrusting out his hand. Sometimes, he tells me, if he rings a bell and finds a woman who is not a Conservative, and conversation is flagging, he just says, 'Oh well, never mind. What about a quick snog?'

This, he says, almost always goes down well, though I am not quite sure whether to believe him.

I meet a copper in the South Oxfordshire village of Kidmore End, who recounts the irritation involved in filling out a handcuff form. You snap a pair of plastic cuffs on a drugs dealer to stop him heading off or causing trouble; but the first thing you have to do when you get back to the station is fill in some long account of what you have done.

(I used this point several times in my speeches; in fact, I made such a thing of it that Marina, in a spirit of independent leftiness, made enquiries of another police officer to find out if it was true. 'Handcuff form?' he allegedly told her. 'Why, there's nothing to it. Done in a jiffy. Nothing I like better, on a slow afternoon, than filling out a handcuff form,' he said. Or so my wife informs me. I merely lay both points of view before you, and continue in my conviction that the police have too much paperwork, and that is a key reason why you see so few of them about.)

In the evening we go canvassing in Woodcote with Christopher Quinton, who sets a blistering pace. As we approach one door a couple of girls come out, get into a fast-looking black car, and start accelerating towards us. I leap out of the way, and one girl, with black lipstick, shouts something about how good it would be if there were 'two less Tory candidates'.

I approach the car, stick my head down near the window, and say, 'You mean two fewer Tory candidates.'

'Hey?' says the girl.

'Not two less, two fewer,' I repeat.

The other girl says something to the girl with black lipstick. Oh, she says.

Huh, she says, engages the gear, and the car snarls away. Later on somebody tells me that one or other of them was a transvestite. Still, that's no reason to be hostile to the Tory party, I would have thought.

* * *

Let me give a piece of advice to any candidate being interviewed by A. A. Gill, the chap from the *Sunday Times*. Just let him get on with it. Allow him to stitch you up. It's in his nature. Above all, don't fall into the trap of so many novice politicians (i.e. me) and think you can manipulate him into writing what you want.

Here's Gill at 9 a.m. in the Watlington office, looking pretty exotic. He is wearing pre-faded ironed jeans with sort of winklepicker cowboy boots, and a James Bond white tuxedo. His oiled black curls cling tightly to his delicate skull, and the whole apparition exudes a mixture of tobacco and Dolce & Gabbana Number 5. He is already expressing deep boredom.

He enlarges this into a metropolitan horror at the size of the Henley constituency, and the comparative scarcity of bistros, restaurants, massage-parlours and other civilised amenities. It is clearly my duty to cheer him up. We have the answer. 'You're off canvassing,' says Chris, just for a change, and we make for the lovely village of Tetsworth. Anthony and I lead the way in the Sirocco, Gill following with his photographer, both of them looking as cynical as Diogenes. As we go, I optimistically sketch out Gill's piece in my head: CANDIDATE STICKS TO OLD METHODS – 'Nothing beats knocking on doors,' says Johnson; or perhaps, TORY CANDIDATE MARVELS AT CONSTITUENTS' GARDENS. 'I love the smell of lavender in the morning,' says Johnson. 'It smells of victory.' That's the stuff to give the troops, I think. That's what Gill's *Sunday Times* readers will be expecting – simple, from-the-shoulder stuff. Gill has other ideas.

Tetsworth is quiet, as you might expect at 11 a.m. on a weekday morning: here the clicking of shears, there the hum of a mower or the trundle of a pram. But we do find several people, and successfully canvass their opinions, none of which, curiously, finds its way into the article which is eventually produced by Alphonse Adrian Gill, or whatever A. A. stands for. His angle is altogether different. He finds nothing to admire in our industry or use of old-fashioned methods. He just thinks it is preposterous to be 'on the knocker' at 11 a.m., and he asserts that we meet only eight electors in three hours.

It is the same when we come across a baby. I know the rules with babies. It is a good idea to kiss them. They smell nice; the gesture is taken as a sort of compliment by the parents, and I have briefly pecked a couple during the course of the campaign. But you don't kiss them unless you are specifically so ordered by their mothers. So I merely lean over this baby and guess that its age is one month. You might think I deserved some credit for being able to get that right. But no. Gill merely says that I look at the baby 'as if it were Sunday lunch'.

And so it goes on. In the pub I have what I think is rather a learned conversation with a gamekeeper about pheasants. According to A. A. Gill, I show inadequate knowledge of raptors, and ask a gauche question about the number of pheasants he has. To trip me up, he then asks what sort of soil they have in these parts and lovingly reports me as saying, 'Um, oh Lor', flinty, muddy, chalky, bouillabaisse, I don't know ...'

Over a garden gate we have a valuable discussion with one elector on my position on Third World debt and pollution by Shell in the Ogoni delta of Nigeria. Gill describes this as 'surreal'.

By the time we part, after a torrid interview in another pub, my efforts to spin Gill have been a total failure. He produces a portrait of shambling buffoonery, illustrated by a picture of the candidate screwing up his eyes against the sun like a village idiot, and surmounted by the headline, IT'S BORIS, THE WORST POLITICIAN IN THE WORLD.

You can't really fault him, though. He didn't take a note, and yet the quotations are all fine. It's an amusing, well-structured piece. Never forget how difficult this kind of journalism is, since it consists of making something out of nothing. If anything – what can I say to annoy the old boy? – he's been rather too kind.

Thursday 24 May

Ding dong. 'Hello, good morning, sorry to trouble you, I just wondered if I could introduce myself. I'm standing to be your local MP, and I wondered if I could count on your—'

'I know exactly who you are, and no, sorry, you'll have to forgive me if I end the conversation there, because otherwise I am afraid I might say something offensive.'

According to Central Office guidelines you should immediately pull out at this point. There is no point in whipping up further animosity.

But wait. Here is the man's wife, peeping behind him and smiling. What about you, madam?

'Well, I don't know,' she smiles. 'I only know you as the chap in the paper waving the mace and eating cakes in the shape of a hat.'

Let me explain about the hat. When you write a newspaper column you have to stick your neck out from time to time. It's part of the job. The readers want predictions. You supply them. William Rees-Mogg is a master of this. Mystic Mogg, as he is known, has predicted twelve of the last two recessions, and once opined in *The Times*, shortly after the Korean Airlines jumbo jet KAL 007 disappeared from radar screens over Sakhalin Island, that the explosion was the result of metal fatigue.

The convention, when you make such a blooper, is to ignore it. Forge on. Write an equally trenchant column next week denouncing Russian aggression and paranoia. To do anything else, according to long-established rules of British journalism, would 'shake public confidence in the press'. What, though, if you are not just a journalist but a would-be politician? What if you make a gaffe so egregious that there is no way the reader can possibly forget it?

In the spring of 2001 politics was dominated by the linked questions of the government's handling of the foot and mouth epidemic, and the timing of the election. Compared to the Dutch, who managed to stamp out the disease within weeks, MAFF seemed Neronian in its apathy. Blair did not become directly involved for many weeks; and the accusation was that Labour was just hoping that the whole business would blow over. Ministers had bad motives in trying to minimise the crisis, it was thought, because they were determined not to prejudice their chances of calling an election on 3 May. The advertising was pre-paid; indeed, some Labour ministers had already booked their holidays shortly afterwards. Hardly any parliamentary business was due to be transacted. The economy was ticking over nicely. If they missed their chance in May, so the reasoning ran, Blair and co. would have to wait until the autumn, and then the economy might be slowing down.

So what would Tony do? Would he take seriously the plight of the countryside, where the slaughter policy was producing hideous pyres of animals, and was still beyond the capabilities of the vets and even of the army? Or would he give precedence to Labour's electoral necessities? It had all the makings of a first-class political dilemma. If he went ahead on 3 May, it would be seen as a metropolitan snub to rural people, some of whom might not even have the pleasure of being canvassed by their candidate, since the restrictions prevented anyone coming on to the farms. If he delayed, he might miss his opportunity – in a metaphor no one hesitated to use – to cull the Tories at the same time. Night after night the British people were treated to TV images of death on the farm, followed by Andrew Marr in Downing Street relating, with ever more brilliant use of metaphor, the Prime Minister's wrestlings with his conscience. Even in South Oxfordshire, where there has not yet been, thank heavens, a confirmed outbreak, the question aroused strong feeling. 'I don't see how they can even think of having an election now,' fumed Orpie the pig farmer.

The Tory papers were saying the same. Tory spokesmen were making the case for delay. And yet the *Sun*, which was backing Labour, and which was directly plugged into Alastair Campbell, fought back with sledgehammer rhetoric. 'It HAS to be May 3,' said its editorial column, shortly after revealing 'exclusively' that this was Blair's preferred date. Anything else would be a sign of panic. It would send out the worst possible signal to the world, said the *Sun*. Tony Blair is a GOOD MAN, said the *Sun*. He is RIGHT. The election MUST happen on May 3, the *Sun* told its apathetic readers, and it WILL. Alastair Campbell would not dream, surely, of misleading Trevor Kavanagh, the *Sun*'s political editor, I reasoned; and so, on 26 March, I pronounced. If the election does not take place on May 3, I said, I will eat my hat, garnished with bacon from Heddon on the Wall, scene of the outbreak.

A few days later it was announced that the local elections, and therefore the general election, were being put off till 7 June. Blair had climbed down, found a compromise date, and my position was tricky. The *Telegraph*'s woman in Heddon on the Wall was deputed to buy some bacon. A reader sent in a small blue bobble hat, which she had knitted for the occasion. There was nothing for it but to go on the *Today* programme and munch the thing. Jim Naughtie told his listeners in Henley to look out for a chap with straw-coloured hair and bits of wool hanging out of his mouth.

And yet still the readers of the *Daily Telegraph*,

who tend to be sticklers in every respect, were not satisfied. It wasn't clear to them that the bobble hat had actually been consumed (it wasn't: you try it. It makes you retch). The tone of the correspondence began to heat up.

I'd said in black and white that I'd eat my hat if the election were postponed. The election had been postponed. Was I a man of my word, or not? The *Henley Standard* eventually came to my rescue and baked me a cake in the shape of a boater, which I wore briefly on my head and then ate with the children. This, I hope, has more or less discharged my obligations.

I asked John Major, afterwards, whether it was right to admit so publicly that you were wrong, and he said, no, on the whole you should avoid doing it too often. People got fed up, he said. They don't want endless confessions of error. It makes them wonder why they elected you in the first place. He has a point, though the reader may speculate that Mr Major's thinking has been coloured by the endless right-wing demands for an 'apology' for the ERM disaster. My former tutor, Jasper Griffin, took a rosier view. He thought people quite liked it when politicians admitted they were wrong. Just as women are supposed to like it when men show their vulnerability. Not too much, though, one would have thought, in either case. And here's another one, a chap digging his lawn. He voted for us last time, he says, but can't see himself voting for us this time. That is the really worrying thing: the people still peeling away, and no real sign of them flooding back.

'You'll be the same, Boris!' rages a man on a street corner in Thame. 'You'll go down to Westminster, and you'll get yourself a grace and favour flat, and you won't do anything for anybody.'

It is terrifying, how low the motives of politicians are assumed to be. This man genuinely thinks I am doing it to get to the top of the housing list.

Does he really think MPs get free flats? Chris drags me away, before the situation deteriorates. But before we can go far a small, cross-looking woman comes up and says, 'I've got a bone to pick with you.'

'A bone?' I say, noticing the cross round her neck.

'Yes,' she says, and explains. Uh-oh. It's this one again.

The phone rang in the office in Watlington. For a second I hesitated. It would be much better if Chris answered it. What if it was someone who wanted to complain about the candidate? But Chris was out of the room. Hello, said a cultivated voice. I wanted to make some comments about your prospective candidate. Oh yes, I said. Do go on. Well, for a start, she said, he should stop writing about things like Scotland in his *Telegraph* column, and start writing about the issues that matter to the people of Henley. Like the pavements. And parking! Do you know that I have been living here for eight years, and I still do not have a parking permit? And what, may I ask, is he doing going to Fawley Court, which is not in his constituency?

Fawley Court? I said. Yes, she said, with increasing asperity, why is he going to Fawley Court and apologising, when it is not even in his constituency? At this point I came clean, revealed to the lady that she was speaking to the object of her wrath – which, by the way, did nothing to calm her down – and explained my mission to Fawley Court.

You remember that bit in history, where Henry II goes to Canterbury Cathedral, on his knees, scourging himself, in the hope of atoning for the murder of Thomas à Becket? That was very much the spirit in which I went to this lovely riverside house, constructed by Sir Christopher Wren.

Fawley Court is inhabited by the Marian Fathers, eleven Polish monks or friars. One of them is ninety-seven. There is a fascinating museum of Polish history, full of moving tributes to Polish resistance against Nazi and Soviet oppression. One of my guides stunned me by explaining that he had been in that very detachment of Polish cavalry whose name is for ever illuminated in the annals of chivalry, because, in 1939, they were deployed against the German tanks. It was a myth to say that they actually charged the tanks, he said; but if I understood him correctly, Polish horsemen were certainly used against the Panzers, and he was there that black September. In the library, full of unique volumes, students can be found carefully cataloguing the manuscripts. The chapel seems to be in constant use, and the whole place exudes an atmosphere of quiet zeal, scholasticism and religious observance.

Into this tranquillity, shortly after I was selected to contest the Henley seat, intruded Petronella Wyatt, the *Spectator* columnist. It seems she had arrived, in the company of a friend, to inspect the premises; because one of her ancestors was a celebrated interior decorator, also called Wyatt, who had specialised in fireplaces and sconces and what have you back in the eighteenth century.

Anyone who reads Petronella's column will know that it is, in general, a model of benignity. Most of the jokes are at her own expense, or at the expense of her mother, or her mother's dog, or her assorted Hungarian relatives. Not one of her legions of admirers would call her a polemicist, or a frother at the gills. A typical Wyatt column consists of a meditation on Great Room Service Mix-Ups of the Eighteenth

Century, or whether the story of Neil and Christine Hamilton is suitable for opera. This time, however, she threw a small bomb.

She decided that she didn't like the look of Fawley Court, or possibly that her ancestor's efforts were not displayed to best advantage. Ugh, her piece said, in summary: hideous, hideous, hideous; and added, for good measure, some fantastical abuse of the present inhabitants. We were deluged with letters of protest – from Polish brotherhoods around the world, from local people who felt affection for Fawley Court, and from someone who signed himself Miles Norfolk, and who felt that the *Spectator* should jolly well apologise in the most crawling terms.

It was only after a while that we guessed that this must be the Duke of Norfolk, Britain's top Catholic; though Ann Sindall, my brilliant secretary, was scathing about his apparent modesty. 'Eee oop,' she said, since she comes from Barnsley, 'I'm going to address the letter to Mr Norfolk, whatever you say.'

But what fuelled my natural paranoia, as a parliamentary candidate, was the explicit message – or threat – in some of the letters. Mr Johnson, they said, you should realise that Fawley Court is in your constituency (it isn't, as it turned out – only part of the grounds is in the Henley seat). Some of your constituents will not be happy that you should represent them, while you allow this kind of thing to be printed in your magazine. It would be a good thing, they went on, if you printed a long apology, or showed some other sign of contrition.

Well, I could see what they wanted. They wanted me to sack Wyatt for this outrageous insult to a modest and innocent institution. And since I am a ruthless sort of chap, who believes in considering all the options, I briefly wondered whether to gratify their blood-lust; but only very briefly.

Wyatt had been rude, but all columnists are entitled to their opinions. And anyway, the last time there was some mention of sacking Petronella, I received the most extraordinary letters, not so much from her fans as from their wives. 'Dear Mr Johnson,' said one from the home counties, 'My husband read that you were about to get rid of P. Wyatt, and let out a kind of death-rattle over the cornflakes. I beg you to think again.'

So I wrote letters to all the Fawley Court protesters, pointing out that I had been on holiday when the piece was printed, and had not read it before it went in (a cowardly point, which cut no ice with anyone). And I added how much I hoped to visit Fawley Court soon, to see it for myself.

So I did, and if you want me to arbitrate, I will say that Petronella was in one sense right: the place does not look exactly as Wren, Grinling Gibbons and Wyatt left it. On the other hand, it seemed to me that there was quite a lot to be said for the establishment and its cloistered monkish charm, which our columnist had unaccountably omitted. So I parted from the Marian Fathers with an *Exxon Valdez* of oil poured on troubled waters. And there matters should have rested. Except that I had made the mistake of revealing my mission to Tom Boyle, the Woodward-and-Bernstein of the *Henley Standard*. He produced a piece on the lines of BORIS GROVELS AT FAWLEY – TORY CANDIDATE IN HUMBLE PIE BID.

Which only served, of course, to make matters worse.

Why didn't I sack Petronella on the spot? demanded the woman in Thame. How dare I solicit her vote without firing the woman? and so on.

At which point, I am afraid to say, I decided that enough was enough. I disliked her tone. It would be quite wrong if, as editor of a magazine, I took action against a valued columnist simply to salve some embarrassment she had caused me in my capacity as a parliamentary candidate. I had been to see the Marian Fathers; apologised; that was it. Well, she said, it wasn't good enough, and we both stalked off in a huff.

The whole thing was nonsense, but it was nonsense of my making. Max Hastings, my former editor, has given me many good pieces of advice, but the best was about making goofs. I had somehow confused Holy Trinity Brompton with the Brompton Oratory and, again, provoked a certain amount of Catholic anger. 'If you make a goof,' said Max, 'the great thing to do is shut up about it, and everyone will forget it.' Or as Denis Healey put it, if in hole, stop digging.

WEEK THREE

Polls: They're Not Getting Better

Hooray Henley

Friday 25 May

MORI POLL IN THE TIMES PUTS LABOUR ON 55, TORIES ON 30. Unbelievably awful. The hostility to William is very depressing.

We're sitting on the terrace of the Angel on the River pub, and the light is playing on the Thames, the swans are swanning around, and the whole scene is just too lovely. Knackered after canvassing in Henley North, I have broken the no-alcohol rule and knocked back a pint of bitter shandy.

Now I look around me, and understand why for more than a century this town has been identified with a mix of pleasures: water, and alcohol, and athletic exertion, and sunlight, and filmy dresses, and funny hats. This is how it struck John Betjeman in 1902, during the reign of Edward VII, and the continuity is striking.

Plash of sculls! And pink of ices!
And the inn-yards full of ostlers, and the barrels
running dry,
And the baskets of geraniums
Swinging over river gardens
Led us to the flowering heart of England's willow-
cooled July.

Betjeman is right. The place is a fit subject for poetry. He goes on to describe the Brakspear's brewery down the way; which was, as I say, a conspicuous element of my selection. In fact, it was about the most convincing evidence I could supply (apart from having been educated 'in Oxfordshire') that they were looking at a local man. One of the most enjoyable and productive days was spent in the winter, touring the brewery and discovering how they do it.

First you need malt, explained the chief brewer, as we wandered past the ancient vats. Looking like gigantic timbered daleks, gorgeously modernised with gleaming aluminium. I bet you don't even know what malt is. It is barley seeds, soaked in water. You soak them in water until they are on the point of germination; and then, just when the little shoots are thinking of making a break for it, you roast them. If you want the type of malt they use to make Guinness or other types of stout, you roast them in a coffee-grinder-affair until they are black.

You then shove the malt in fresh water, which in Brakspear's case is to be found in a well beneath the brewery. This is why William Henry Brakspear chose the site in 1779. Then you add sugar and yeast, and you have a brown fluid called 'wort'. This looks like beer, with a few foreign bodies in it, and tastes sweet, as all the sugar has not yet turned to alcohol.

The wort then spends a week in the vat, and the yeast gets to work, and then they do something called 'dropping', where they drop the stuff from one vat to another. I am afraid I didn't quite get this bit, but that may be because it is some sort of commercial secret. It is Brakspear's unique selling point that their beer has been 'double-dropped'.

More knowledgeable fans of Brakspear's beer also say that its taste is famously hoppy, or full of hops. I was very pleased, therefore, when we sat down to lunch, and I saw a little greenish, leafy object floating in my pint.

'That's some hop,' I said, and we all agreed, and got on with our steak and kidney pie. Outside on the river-meadows it had begun to snow, and it was altogether a scene of Dickensian cosiness.

'Wait a minute,' said the chief brewing technician, who had been staring at my hop. 'Could I have a look at that?'

I fished it out. He stared at it in some bafflement.

'This isn't a hop,' he said at length. 'It's a caper from the smoked salmon.' Everyone laughed. Hoppy days, eh?

But now it's summer, and soon it will be the regatta. The tents are being prepared, and in a few weeks one of the great emblematic English events will take place. People often ask me whether I know the British Olympic demigods, who row at Henley, and I am proud to say that I do, a tiny bit.

I rose to my feet. 'Stand up!' said a voice, and then another. Oi, I thought to myself. I may be only five feet ten and a bit, but since when has that been small? 'Stand up,' yelled the room full of 200 rowers, most of them well over six foot, and pretty plastered, and very pleased with this witticism. Somewhat stung, and able to think of nothing more crushing than 'But I am standing up,' I began.

It was the annual dinner of the Leander Club, and I had Matthew Pinsent on my left, and two down, on my right, Steve Redgrave, as well as Cracknell and Foster, the two other members of the Oarsome Foursome who had won the coxless fours gold medal in Sydney. I was on first, the guest of honour, for heaven's sake, to be followed by Pinsent and the chairman of the club. I did my best. I'd been scribbling throughout dinner, having driven like fury through the rain from London, and I reckoned I had about six minutes' worth of waffle.

They liked my line – that Leander was not merely the heart of rowing, but the epicentre of the greatest British aquatic triumph since Trafalgar. Several of them, pink-tied, pink-socked, pink-nosed and, for all I know, pink-cami-knickered, stood up and applauded, swaying and waving their glasses. They listened generously to some lame jokes about catching more crabs on the river at school than I did later at university – and certainly more crabs than there were, Mr President, in the otherwise excellent crab bisque ha ha haaaarrgh. I congratulated them on bringing back a significant quantity of bullion to Britain, almost making up for all the gold flogged off cheap by Gordon Brown ho ho ho.

But it was only when Pinsent took the mike that a great truth struck me about English public life, and the comparative importance of my trade and his. To look at them on the telly, you wouldn't think they were specially big, the British Olympic rowers. They don't appear to bulge like boxers or weightlifters, when seen from a distance. But when they are looming over you, in dinner jackets, and folding their enormous thumbs around yours as you shake hands, you have a sense of what vast, cantilevered beasts they are. I guess the tallness is vital to the physics of rowing, because it's the long legs, straightening explosively, which make the oar sweep so fast through the water; and it is when you hear a chap like Pinsent speaking, and watch the audience reaction, that you feel your littleness. What are we politicians and journalists? Just parasites, epiphytes upon our national culture. How trivial is everything we achieve next to the personal Everests these chaps scale, in endurance and resilience and self-discipline. The public realises this, and that is why the vast majority of newspaper readers probably move straight on past the columnists to the sports pages.

Pinsent spoke in his basso profundo for twenty minutes, without much of a note. He told dirty jokes in a modest and self-deprecating sort of way. He painted a picture of the morning of the contest: he hadn't had anything to eat because he was so nervous, in spite of his coach's instruction. I'd been expecting some kind of dur-brain. I remembered the shouts of 'Row-er' at school, synonymous with dunce. Pinsent was nothing of the kind. He was fluent, amiable, and obviously highly intelligent. I expect he'll be on all sorts of boards, a quangocrat, a peer. Did I feel small? I am sixteen stone. I played rugby for school and Balliol, and even for the Oxford freshmen's XV. But in the face of that kind of athleticism, small is what I felt.

⋆ ⋆ ⋆

A man comes out from under a car in Shiplake. He is covered with grease, but that is not why he is so annoyed. He gets covered with grease for a living. I have just asked him to vote Tory, and he hardly meets my eye, he finds the idea so irritating.

'I've always voted Tory, and I voted Tory last time,' he says. 'But I'm certainly not voting for you lot after what happened last time.'

Hang on a minute, I say. Last time we had an election, Labour won by a stonking landslide. You can't blame us for what Labour did next, can you? You surely don't blame the Tories for Labour's tax hikes on petrol, pensions and everything else?

'No, I don't,' says the mechanic. 'But that's not the point, is it? I blame you for what didn't happen.'

Huh? I say.

'You had these advertisements before the last election saying that interest rates would go up if Labour won. So of course I went out and got a fixed rate mortgage, and so did a lot of people I know.'

Uh-oh, I'm thinking.

'And we reckon we've all lost a fair bit of money, because we believed your advertisements.'

By this time, as you might imagine, I'm feeling fairly dreadful. All these advertisements are mendacious, at election time. The Lib Dems are running some utter baloney about what the Tories plan to do to the NHS. But what if it's true that we went big on the threat to interest rates, and caused innocent people to lose money?

It's the double whammy, isn't it? The Tories promise not to raise taxes in 1992, and then find themselves obliged to do so. And they warn that Labour will put up interest rates in 1997, and are made to look fools when it doesn't happen.

Saturday 26 May

I'm on the M40, heading back to see the family. Sometimes you're bombing along a motorway, and the traffic suddenly slows. Hello hello hello, you say to yourself, what's going on here, then? And after a while you see your answer: there's a police car dawdling along at seventy, and everybody feels they ought to show a smidgeon of respect for the law. Like a bunch of sheep, they cluster about the sheepdog, with an absurd pretence of piety. They have seat-belts fastened, hands on the wheel at ten to two, mobiles in their crotches and butter-wouldn't-melt-in-mouth expressions on their faces.

Ahoy there, officer, they are saying to themselves. Look at me, sir. I am in compliance with the speed regulations. Oh yes, they wheedle, as they begin to inch past the police car at seventy-one or seventy-two or seventy-three m.p.h., you couldn't say that I was speeding, could you? And so it goes on until they are two or three furlongs in front, and everyone feels the proprieties have been observed. At which point the toe pushes down on the throttle and *yeeee-ow*.

That is how almost everybody behaves on motorways, I am sorry to say – everyone, that is, except a group of goody-goodies who seem to have a reverence for the fuzz. Who are they? you may ask as you scorch past in your Alfa or your Beemer. Who are these saps who stick at seventy m.p.h.? I will tell you. They are probably candidates for Parliament; they are prospective MPs who are suddenly overwhelmed by feelings of responsibility.

Here I am on the M40, rushing back to see everyone in London on a Saturday morning. Under normal circumstances I would be going at a pretty fair lick. But today I hesitate, and I feel the weight of my new position.

The police may be there to enforce the law; but, my God, aren't MPs there to make the law? If we don't obey it, who will? It's not just that you don't want the embarrassment of being done for speeding, or not paying your car tax, or talking on your mobile as you cycle the wrong way down a one-way street. You feel – and this may sound utterly ridiculous – that you are aspiring to be part of the same set-up as them, the great empire of law.

All would-be MPs traditionally express their gratitude to the police. But I want to pay a particular tribute to the two officers in jerseys who helped push my Ferrari 456 Maranello off the fast lane of the M40, at the height of the rush hour, when I had run out of petrol. It was an act of incompetence for which I deserved a heavy fine. The officers showed great coolness and disregard for their own safety, especially since the passing traffic was taking no account of the speed limit.

Sunday 27 May

Gill's article appears, greatly pleasing friend and foe alike. The Lib Dems are so chuffed with the headline that they put it on one of their flyers. Across Goring they are getting through their letter boxes the news that Boris is 'the worst politician in the world'. They add this to other choice Boris headlines.

You may think I bang on about this too much, but do you not feel that these Lib Dems are the Jekyll and Hyde of British politics? Charlie Kennedy comes over as earnest and well-meaning; and the Lib Dems have cunningly positioned themselves to attract the votes of some of the most earnest and most well-meaning people in Britain. I ask one woman why she is going to vote Lib Dem, and she says it is because they are 'a party of high morals and principles'.

You could have fooled me. They have the luxury of offering policies they will never be called upon to implement, and, at the risk of sounding priggish, they resort to deceit. I hear of Lib Dem leaflets in the West Country which give the false impression that the Lib Dems are more Euro-sceptic than either of the two other parties. 'The pound – you decide,' they say, before making the ridiculous claim that 'both Labour and the Conservatives have refused the public a referendum'.

In Thame market I meet a man who has just walked by the Lib Dem stall. He assures me with a glassy stare that he is going to vote Lib Dem, because they are the only ones who are absolutely sure to keep the pound.

No they're not, you say. Yes they are, he says, robotically. Has he, perhaps, been hypnotised? It is very hard not to conclude that he has somehow derived this impression from talking to the Lib Dems, and that they are therefore guilty of the most monstrous misrepresentation.

Asylum-seekers

Monday 28 May

We have another good turn-out in Sonning Common, with at least 100 people in the audience. But the most important man there is a reporter.

He covered the Abdication. He reported the war in Abyssinia. He covered the Munich crisis, and went to meet Chamberlain when the Prime Minister arrived back at Heston aerodrome and waved his piece of paper. He fought in the war, served in the Cabinet, and is the head of the profession of journalism. He is W. F. Deedes. And now he's turned out to write a report on my campaign. What a thing, eh?

Bill was elected MP for Ashford, where his family has lived for ages, in 1950. He is particularly good on how to suck up to dogs. When we meet a labrador in Binfield Heath, he instructs me in the art of shaking a dog's hand. In fact, Bill goes in for some pretty heavy petting. 'You cannot go wrong,' says Bill, 'by befriending the dog. The owner will remember it. He will vote for you.'

Tonight's news is full of race riots, blazing cars in Bradford, and endless jabber about the Tory position on race. Here at the meeting in Sonning Common are some people from Amnesty International, who have come specially to duff me up for my party's (alleged) stance. It's been happening quite a lot during the campaign, particularly when we meet young, idealistic audiences.

Excuse me, said the girl. I can see her now. Tense, white-faced. I couldn't swear that her nostrils were flared, because she was sitting about twenty feet away from me; but she was pretty fired up.

You Tories, she said – and I paraphrase – you Tories are just playing the race card, aren't you? You're stoking up these base feelings against asylum-seekers, the most vulnerable people in society. And the nape of my neck prickled.

So far the meeting had been going tolerably well. But the mood of such gatherings can turn as irrevocably as milk in the sun. Aha, the students were thinking: a Tory. Oh yes. Immigrant-bashers, that's what they are. Come on, fatso, defend yourself and your party. And feeling a bit flustered, I did.

Now look here, I said, or words to that purpose; you can't hang that one on me. You can't call me a racist, no sir, not when my own family is the produce of more than one country, as they say on those pots of honey; not when we Johnsons have enough nationalities in our immediate inheritance to make up a UN peacekeeping force. Indeed no, I cried …

But my questioner wasn't standing for it. Up shot her hand again.

Come on, Mr would-be politician, she said, your party is trying to make political capital out of bogus asylum-seekers. Many people find the use of that word offensive. How do you plead?

And I began to think of a way of finding, Blair-like, some papier-mâché disguise for our disagreement.

You mean, I said, that the word bogus is offensive?

Uh-huh, said the girl, and about thirty other students of Henley College nodded as one.

Right, I said. Bogus. Offensive, eh? Hmm, I thought, and then I gave up the effort of compromise. But they are bogus, for heaven's sake – or at least a great many of them are.

There was a sucking-in of breath. Oh come off it, I pleaded, I honestly, sincerely, had nothing against these people. They had travelled for thousands of miles, in conditions of great discomfort, to seek a new life in a country where they could not even speak the language. They were often the victims of racketeers and, in the most tragic instance, they were left to suffocate in containers.

But the awful fact was that not all of them, by any means, could be called asylum-seekers, in that they were not in fear of death or persecution in the country from which they had come. In an average year about 80 per cent of asylum applications were rejected, I said ...

Yeah, said the girls, not even bothering to put their hands up this time, but how do you know that those cases deserved to be rejected? How do you know it wasn't just the Home Office who turned them down on some technicality?

Oh for heaven's sake, I said. I'll give you an example.

A few weeks ago we were trying to teach the children to ride bicycles in a churchyard in darkest N7. I was wandering back to the park bench, where I had left a pair of roller skates, and noticed that a family of four had sat down. The father had borrowed the skates, and had just finished lacing them on his little boy.

Fine, fine, I said, as I drew level. Go ahead and borrow them. This chap was plainly ambitious for his son's roller-skating career, towing him along in spite of the look of terror on the kid's face. At last he twigged that the skates were ours, and started taking them off.

'No problem, no problem,' he said.

No, no, go ahead, I tried to insist, but the kid was whimpering as though he had had enough coaching. The family looked Turkish, though there was something Slavic about the language. The dad was wearing a pair of Noddy Holderish flares.

'Kosovo,' he said. 'Me Kosovo.' Ah, I said. I knew Kosovo a bit. The woman beamed at me, and I noticed that she had several heads of roses in her hands. In fact, call me an old killjoy, but it sort of bugged me to see that the kids were wandering around the churchyard – infested with tramps, but still pretty – and decapitating the blooms. The tarmac beneath the bench was strewn with pink, yellow and red petals.

They were Albanians, and they'd come from Mitrovica in September 1999. It had been three days and three nights in 'camion', he said; pitch-black in the back; the space shared with about ten other people; a trip so bad they had given the boy, seven, and the girl, three, Valium to silence their wails. He wasn't sure of the route, but believed it might have been from Macedonia via Italy. They had changed lorry once, at a place he didn't recognise, and finally found the doors opened by the police in London. The whole trip had cost DM7000 (more than £2000).

He was full of praise for the London police. They asked him where he was from. He told them he was from Kosovo. They directed him to the social services. He was also content with the education being offered his seven-year-old, at a school over the road, and with the general understanding shown by the social services. He was less complimentary, however, about the 'hotel'. He pointed across Liverpool Road at a large, modern, red-brick affair, with what looked like a wire fence around the walls. There was only one kitchen for thirteen families, he said, and his wife was three months pregnant with their third child, at which point she smiled and patted her stomach ...

Now I didn't say all of this to the students in Henley. I gave them an abbreviated account; but I could see that they were not satisfied. There was a sucking of teeth and a rolling of eyes.

Yeah? they said. And what point are you making?

Well, the point I want to make, I said, is that it was not at all clear to me, prima facie, that this chap deserved asylum. Here he is, from Kosovska Mitrovica, a place where there are still, admittedly, some Serbs, but which is under KFOR protection, and where the Serbs have had very much the worse of it during the last year.

We have expended vast quantities of western treasure to ensure that Kosovo Albanians are safe from persecution. My new friend did not flee Kosovo while Slobodan Milosevic was purging the area. He did not flee during the NATO bombing, when Slobo's thugs were torching Albanian homes. He put his family into a lorry three months after NATO had invaded and pacified the province – an operation I had witnessed and reported.

In other words, I could see no very good reason why a Kosovo Albanian should have been given asylum at that stage, and I could see no very good reason why he should not be sent back …

It would be nice to say that this lucid account turned aside the wrath of the Henley students. It did not.

Could I not see, they demanded, that it must have been very traumatic to live through the Serb pogroms and the NATO bombings? Was I made of stone?

Of course not, I said, and in desperation, played my ace. Here is a fact that will stun you, I announced: I am the grandson of an asylum-seeker.

Which is perfectly true. My great-grandfather was a man called Ali Kemal, a Turk. He was the only one of my recent ancestors, so far as I can discover, who was both a journalist and a politician. He ran a small and vaguely conservative magazine. He also rose high in Ottoman politics while not, alas, showing much flair for self-protection. In about 1921 he decided that the would support the last sultan, Abdulhamid, against Kemal Atatürk, the father of the modern Turkish nation. In fact, while serving in the Sublime Porte as Interior

Minister (he was the Michael Howard or Jack Straw of his day) he signed an arrest warrant for Atatürk.

This proved unwise. My great-grandfather was ambushed while in a barber's shop in Izmit, near Istanbul, beaten to death by a bunch of pro-Atatürk thugs and stuck in a tree. His son, my father's father, was called Osman Ali, though he changed his name to Johnson when he arrived here, with his mother, courtesy of the Royal Navy.

Now that, I thought, should shut them up. I should not have been so naïve.

Hmmm, they sniffed, and you could see them calculating the merits of the respective cases. Why should the UK authorities have admitted the son of the Turkish Interior Minister, and not some poor Albanian family from war-torn Mitrovica?

In fact, you could see them thinking, was there not a case – at least under my own argument – for sending Johnson back to Turkey?

It didn't matter what I said or did. The Tories were under suspicion of whipping up racial feeling, and nothing one said could allay that.

Look here, said another one of the students, warming to the attack, what about this John Townend? Shouldn't William Hague have expelled him from the party? And for a second or two, as I pondered my answer, I was on the verge of making matters worse.

Readers may have forgotten the case of Mr Townend, a choleric Yorkshire-born MP who electrified the campaign by saying something about a 'mongrel' race. The spat began with a speech by Robin Cook, which was surely contrived to tempt some Tory to error. 'Isn't it just maaaahvellous,' said Robin Cook, 'that the nation's favourite dish is chicken tikka masala? Doesn't that just make you feel all warm and gooey inside about our maaahvellous multicultural society?'

Actually, I think Robin Cook had a point. My optimistic view of immigration is that it will eventually produce a new syncretic British culture, absorbing the best from each immigrant population (like chicken tikka masala, which was famously invented in Leeds, and which calls for a pint of Campbell's tomato soup). And I think this would be better than a 'multicultural' society of mutually segregated ethnic groups, each with a vast apparatus of lawyers and lobbyists, and an eternal feeling of grievance.

It is also possible that John Townend was playing to the racist brigade – in which case his remark was disgraceful.

But somehow I felt an instinctive temptation to defend Townend. Nasty comments were made in the *Guardian* to the effect that he was a former accountant (boo) and wore an overcoat with a velvet collar (hiss).

Hang about, one thought, just press rewind for a second. What did the old Yorkshire terrier actually say?

He demanded to know whether Robin Cook was saying that the British had long been a 'mongrel' race; and that, frankly, is a very interesting question. There is an unsayable truth (actually, like so many unsayable truths, it has been printed in the *Spectator*) about the present immigration: namely that it is different from any other period open to our observation. A great deal of balls has been talked about the 'waves' of immigration, from Romans, Vikings, Jutes, Angles, Saxons, Normans, Jews, Huguenots and what have you, as though Britain's ethnic composition were in a state of perpetual flux. No, says David Coleman, a reader in demography at Oxford, that is very far from the case. If you study the genetic make-up of the British, the bloodstock has been stable and homogeneous for the last 1000 years. What is new is the level of post-war immigration, which, as we all know, is about to produce Asian majorities in Leeds and Bradford.

In other words, Townend was right, in his *verkrampte* way, to see a flaw in Robin Cook's argument. Britain might or might not be becoming a mongrel nation, and that might or might not be a good thing. But it was a lie to suggest that the British had always been in just such a state of rapid ethnic diversification.

Yeah, I was about to say to the students; just think, before you condemn Townend as a bigot, that he may have a point about the demographics …

And then, perhaps, some divinity invisibly whispered wisdom in my ear, because I remembered that discussions about race and immigration are unfair. They are conducted in a binary framework. No subtlety is allowed, and all points are sifted for their essential tendency one way or the other. You are either on the side of the immigrant; or else you are a reactionary and a Powellite and a nose-caliper-wielding believer in the racial theories of Houston Stewart Chamberlain.

What these students wanted to know was whether I was a goodie or a baddie on Race. Since I am a goodie, I made clear my disapproval of Townend; but also said that it would be excessive to expel him from the party, especially since he was in any event retiring.

Fudge! Fudge! Great geysers of molten fudge. And all because you can't say anything about immigration without being accidentally or wilfully misconstrued. By the end of the election campaign the Tories had lost the battle on asylum-seekers. Any criticism of Labour's handling of the issue became 'playing the race card'.

But which party was really liberal and compassionate? One Sunday Marina and I went to celebrate South Africa Freedom Day in Trafalgar Square. All the toadying Labour ministers were there, glugging back the champagne. Here was Dome supremo Falconer, gassing so loudly with Geoff Hoon during the High Commissioner's speech that he was asked to shut up by a brace of Zulu warriors with assegais and leopard-skin accessories. There were Chris Smith and Baroness Jay, the one whispering to the other and pointing when we walked in. Here, for some reason, was Martin McGuinness, blushing and gloating, no doubt, about penetrating the British establishment.

And there was Blair, on the platform with Nelson Mandela. About the only redeeming feature of the whole affair was that Blair's microphone failed to work, which allowed me to lead, I am not ashamed to say, a gentle chorus of booing, taken up by the ganja-puffing crowd. Barbara Follett, the long-lashed and rebellious Labour MP for Stevenage, turned round and gave me a look which I took to be approval – and quite right. They were right to boo.

Here were the Labour hierarchs, luxuriating in their feelings of chic and cool and cred, bathed in the aura of Mandela's greatness, and making the only Tories present – me and Cheryl Gillan – feel faintly out of place. And what policy were they themselves running towards the asylum-seekers?

They were letting them arrive in droves, but then treating them abominably. The incomers were not allowed to work. They were given a miserable £36.40 per week on which to live, payable in vouchers reminiscent of the ghetto. They were dispersed throughout the country, and kept in conditions like the ones my friend from Mitrovica described. They were the objects of suspicion and sometimes persecution by the natives. And at the end of months, if not years, of legal monkeying around, 80 per cent of them were told that they were not, after all, eligible to stay. To cap it all, the very ministers who were boogying on down to Trafalgar Square had simultaneously been party to Jack Straw's new Home Office guidelines, which amount to a specific discrimination against coloured as opposed to white would-be immigrants.

Where was the humanity in that? Me, I am in favour of controlled immigration. The country needs it. If people are really so determined that they will uproot themselves and pay £2000 to travel in the back of a lorry, the chances are that they will make a go of it. If you were really worried about scroungers, you could perhaps stipulate that they could not draw benefits for a year after arrival.

But let's stop the nonsense about 'asylum'. It ought to be possible for a candidate at an election to find fault with the procedures without being accused of playing the race card.

It ought to be possible to use the word 'bogus'

without being accused of whipping up ill-feeling against foreigners.

It ought to be. But it isn't.

For supper I go into the fish and chip shop in Watlington. To my amazement, my host throws wide his arms and insists on giving me an enormous free portion of haddock and about a kilo of chips. 'You are the greatest man in the world,' he says. I may be slightly exaggerating this quotation, but not much. It is not that he wants to suck up to the Tory candidate; not at all. He is a Serb from Bosnia, and he approved very strongly of my coverage from Belgrade and Kosovo. To anyone who says I should declare my freebies, including fish and chips, I do so now. The haddock is delicious, and a vast improvement on the cheese in the fridge, which is all I have left. According to my friend Heffer, cheese is very dangerous for the arteries, especially Stilton.

Law and Order

Wednesday 30 May

Everyone up in arms because of the Hague as Thatch poster, I mean the one with the Thatch thatch on Hague's head. The *Telegraph* says this is an outrage. I can't see why. It looks like a perfectly reasonable piece of common abuse. Anyone who knows William Hague will tell you that he is very far from his caricature. He is a youthful, humane, cosmopolitan sort of chap. But the Labour Party are entitled to pretend that we are all Thatcher in drag. It's up to us to show we're not.

We're out canvassing for Roy Tudor-Hughes, who is standing for the county council. He can't do much campaigning himself because he is climbing Everest.

This enables the electors to make jokes.

'I tell you what,' says a man leaning on his spade, 'Roy's not the only one with a mountain to climb.'

Thursday 31 May

Terrific timing by Jeffrey Archer. The news breaks that he has paid someone £20,000 to give him an alibi in the Monica Coghlan business. Just the thing for the Tories. Here we are, a week to go, and all the papers can talk about is Tory sleaze. Whatever happened to Labour sleaze?

It was all so different a mere eight months ago. I remember being in the Metropole Hotel's TV studio with the Prime Minister during the last Labour conference. We were on the top floor, with the usual conference vista sea and gulls. He was looking good, his youthful elastic skin still wearing the tan of France and Tuscany. He had a sharp blue suit, a white shirt and a strong red tie. He was on *Breakfast with Frost*, and he was lying his head off.

I was loitering around after doing a paper review with Andrew Rawnsley, who had just produced his magnificent book, exposing the Prime Minister's deceptions in the Ecclestone affair. It was now up to Frost to make the accusations stick. You could tell how tense the position was. There were assorted special branch thugs standing around, with bits of curly-wurly plastic coming out of their ears. Alastair Campbell was sitting like a basilisk in front of me, his eyes flicking restlessly over the scene, and taking notes in a cramped little scrawl.

Remember that we had just had the fuel protest. An NOP poll had put the Tories *ahead* by eight points. Suddenly I thought I understood all Labour's paranoia and control freakery. They were always terrified, because they knew they were phoney, and that it was only a matter of time before someone rumbled them. Would Frost now succeed in impaling Blair on his lies, or would Blair get away with it again?

Time and again, like some lumbering gladiator, Frost closed in on his victim, and every time Blair seemed to slip away, like a greased Christian piglet. At the end, Rawnsley said, excitedly, 'He lied twice.'

But who cared? Can you remember what the lies were about? The trouble with Labour sleaze was that it didn't seem to damage Labour. It either reminded people of Tory sleaze, or inclined them to believe that all politicians were scum. The Labour Party and the Conservative Party have spent so long shelling each other's positions with accusations of sleaze that they are both blasted and cratered like the Somme, and the voter is thoroughly turned off.

'You're all the same!' people groan at me, before shutting the door. 'I'm not voting!' they wail through the letterbox.

Another sweltering day, so hot that one voter has taken her clothes off and is lying in her back garden. She eventually appears, looking blonde, brown and cheerful. Will she vote for us? You betcha. She even lets her towel slip a little at the front. It is such small acts of kindness that keep us going. Later that evening the door opens in another part of the same neck of the woods, and a glass of red wine is thrust wordlessly into my hand. It ought to be more obvious to people that the Tories are broad-minded, fun-loving people. The other day Marina went to the loo in an enormous posh Tory house and emerged reporting that she had found a collection of *Playboys*. They were all bound and organised, she said, with the kind of attention that you might give to your back issues of the *Spectator*. Can you find it in your heart to condemn? I can't. She spent quite a long time, too.

We meet a man who is marketing manager of Walker's Crisps. He's pushing a baby in Goring high street, and my nerves are instantly jangling.

As I have observed before in this account, I believe – perhaps irrationally – that these people are the key to elections. So it's hand out, big smile.

'I'm sorry,' he says, 'but I just think Tony Blair is doing a fantastic job.'

I think you will agree that it is pretty big of me to report that. I do so because there is no limit to the humility that we Tories must show, if we are ever to have a hope of winning office again.

'I've read your leaflet, thank you,' says a woman on the doorstep. 'You talk a lot about crime. What I want to know is what you are actually going to do about it.'

It is true that Chris has produced some election literature which contains a photograph of me talking to Inspector Whitaker outside Henley police station. My arm happens to be thrust forward in a purposeful way, and Whitaker – an extremely nice man – is standing with his hands folded before him, and looking as though he is listening to what I am saying.

'Great!' said Chris. 'It really looks as though you are giving him a piece of your mind.' He captioned the photo, 'Boris Johnson raising concerns with the police'.

Marina, on the other hand, was pretty scathing. Huh, she said, what's all this 'Boris Johnson fights crime' nonsense? What are you going to do that Labour isn't doing? And that, pretty much, was the shape of the debate during the great election of 2001.

It is one of the unedifying features of adversarial politics that the Opposition, in theory, benefits from things going wrong. There are some Tories who believe that the party will not recover until there is a decent recession, and Gordon Brown is shown to have been hubristic in his claim to have gone beyond 'boom and bust'. It is a gloomy way of thinking, but there is, alas, something in it. In the same way, the Opposition should in theory benefit from public dissatisfaction over crime, and that is why all opposition parties – Labour was no exception – will make much of the statistics.

According to the figures, violent crime was rising under Labour, after several years of falling under Iron Mike Howard and other Tories. According to the figures, there were 2500 fewer policemen than when Labour came to power in 1997. This had the makings of a campaign. The Tories ran their famous poster of a hassled-looking woman carrying her shopping bags in a council estate. YOU PAID THE TAXES – WHERE ARE THE POLICEMEN? it said.

And maybe it was just that my cerebrally implanted silicon chip was responding to transmissions from Tory Central Office, but I started to see crime everywhere. When I went to a bring-and-buy sale in Sonning Common, I was amazed to see a burned-out car outside the doctor's surgery. There was a ram-raid in Benson, of all places. Of course, South Oxfordshire is generally safe, but there are still four crimes per day in the Henley area. When I wandered around town with him, Inspector Whitaker had several men off sick, including one who had his head stoved in when attending an armed robbery. Whitaker was particularly pleased that they'd later caught one of the burglars, an Asian who had come in from Reading, and who had made the mistake of raiding the property of a night-club bouncer while the bouncer was on the premises.

Then there was my own experience of crime on the streets of inner-city London. I propped my bike against the primary school gates to say goodbye to the two eldest, turned my back, and – *pow* – it was gone. I wouldn't have minded so much, but it was the second to be stolen in two months, and it was a jolly nice mountain bike. Luckily I spotted it down the road, being ridden by a young black kid; and since he didn't seem to understand the gears I was able to overhaul him by the zebra crossing at Highbury Corner.

'Oi you,' I said, 'get off my ****** bike.'

'What are you talking about?' he shrieked, and then dropped the bike and scarpered down an alleyway.

At the school gates afterwards the young mums were full of praise (why? I hadn't even collared him). 'They watch you, they do. He would have been watching you to see when you were going to put your bike down. He was picking his moment. He might have been watching you for days,' said the one with the blonde hair.

'We were mugged the other day on the bus,' said another mum. 'They followed us on to the bus, and then they robbed us. They withdrew four hundred pounds from our accounts within twenty-five minutes.'

'I'd cut their hands off,' said a third mum.

I report these sentiments for the benefit of anyone who doubts the prevalence of crime in some parts of Britain, and the rage of the people – often on middle to low incomes – who feel that nothing is done to protect them. How many times have we heard from victims of crime that they were told by the police that they were 'too busy to attend', or that there was nothing they could do?

So what, to return to the woman's question, do I propose to do? Well, there's one thing I'd do, I tell her, based on talking to several senior police officers. You can pay for more policemen on the beat, but first you ought to tackle the rampant abuse of long-term sick leave. According to Whitaker, a quarter of his personnel are off on the sick, and about 70 per cent of officers retire on long-term sick leave! She liked that, and closed the door with what I took to be satisfaction.

One potential solution I don't mention, though.

I was stunned, when talking to the Thames Valley Police, to hear their views about drugs and crime. Most of the robberies in the Henley area are committed by people who have come over from Reading; and most of the time they need money to fuel a drugs habit. If you estimate that you need £3000 of goods to buy £300 worth of drugs, that's a lot of burgling you need to do. In a place like Reading most of the crime is committed by twenty to thirty persistent offenders, and they are almost all on drugs. One policeman I talked to seemed to be in no doubt that if you legalised drugs, you would greatly reduce crime. Are the police right, and if so, do politicians have the guts to make this point? Do I? I don't know.

An old woman raises the bus pass question again. Now look here, she says: it costs me £1.80 to go from Chalgrove to Cowley. Are you trying to tell me that is half-fare?

Er, what's the full fare?

It's £3.60.

Well (*whizz, clunk*), that sounds like half-fare, I say. Yes, she says, but they are still making money on it, aren't they?

You sometimes get the impression that no one in this country is allowed to make money if they are involved in health, education or transport.

Here, on the other hand, is a man who cooks in a gastropub, and who seems to have a point. He is talkative and amiable, and kneads his hands together anxiously. His wife goes out to work, and he has to find £750 per month to cover the cost of nursery school.

What am I going to do about it? That is a big bill for a cook.

Well, of course, I bluster, you will be getting back your married couple's allowance, if we get in … but on the specific nursery question … um … ah … no.

We are saying that there are seven days to save the pound. It's a good slogan, but the trouble is that everyone knows there will be a referendum as well. It sounds too much like seven days to save the Tory party.

WEEK FOUR

Election: Over the Top

Ow Ow Ow

Friday 1 June

We are in a garden centre, pursued by journalists, and here is a pretty blonde mother, called Kay Stephenson. She remembers me from Oxford and says she might still conceivably vote for me, for old times' sake, but frankly, my party … !

'You just don't talk to people like me,' she says. 'The front bench … !' she says. Her husband, who runs an engineering firm in Abingdon, is going to vote Labour for the first time in his life, she says. She is a natural Tory, she says, but this time, really, she isn't sure at all …

Oh please, I say. Please, please, please.

Oh all right, she says, at length.

This is how Simon Hoggart of the *Guardian* reported the encounter:

> 'You don't engage me at all. You have too many people in the party who are from a different planet entirely. And you are going to win and be in a morale-destroying minority when you could have a much better time editing the *Spectator*. And what about your wife and children?' Boris groaned, presumably because he suspected she was right on all counts. He ran his fingers through his increasingly manic hair. He must keep a pitchfork in his back pocket for when it needs straightening.

Here we are, I say to the troops, this one is bound to be a Lib Dem. The dwelling we are approaching is a deconsecrated church. I am always filled with a slight gloom by these buildings, testimony as they are to the ebbing of the tide of faith. This one's ecclesiastical past has been half-disguised by various loggias, vines and imaginative architectural features.

Oh yes, I think, as I push open the gate and walk down the path: quite an expensive building, and probably the ritziest in the street. This is Lib Dem territory, all right. I ring the bell. Someone comes.

Pok pok pok pok go her footsteps down what was once the aisle and *pok pok pok* left into what was once the church porch.

The ex-church door opens, slowly. A grey-haired

woman stands there, looking at me through her spectacles. Before I can say a word she shrieks: 'AaaaaAAAAAAARgGGGh!' and the door slams. I turn back and walk out, carefully shutting the gate.

Yup. What did I tell you. Lib Dem, all right.

Sunday 3 June

The last push. Over the top. Do or die. Or both. We have drawn up a brilliant letter to be distributed to every voter. It attacks Labour's failure to deliver on its promises and the deteriorating public services in this country.

Except that for some reason this is printed as – ha ha ha – 'deteriorating pubic services'.

We have all read the damn thing. None of us can escape blame. We all take collective responsibility, particularly me.

We have surprisingly few complaints. One woman apparently rings up and asks what I am going to do to improve her pubic services.

Ho ho ho.

Our 'kindly stop hitting me' policy is hotting up. It is interesting to watch the way information about voter behaviour filters from the doorstep back to campaign HQ, and then generates a new line.

It was about a week ago that I, and presumably

others, first noticed that this 'ow ow ow' approach was being well taken by the electorate. It has long been perfectly obvious that the Tories were due for another caning. So suddenly you switch, by instinct, and try to appeal to the fairness of the punters, their natural support for the underdog.

OK, you say, when you have someone havering on the doorstep. You're right. We're going to get thrashed. But does that mean we should have the living daylights thrashed out of us? Do you really want Blair prancing and swanking and beaming and crowing?

At this, people would suddenly stop, scratch their chins, and say, Yeah, that's true. Hmmm. All the same, Mori gives the Labour Party a twenty-three-point lead.

Monday 4 June

I don't like it at all. I don't like these canvass returns. Too many of the Cs seem to be turning to As – Conservatives turning into Againsts. Not enough of the Ls (Libs) and Ss (Socialists) are turning into Cs.

Chris says I am being paranoid, and that we are doing very well. We are finding masses of Tories. In case you should get the contrary impression, we are being received, overall, with great friendliness and warmth. But will it add up to votes?

One man comes up to me in Thame and says, 'I love you. I think you are going to be the Socrates of the Conservative Party. You are going to come up with the big idea that rescues them.'

Needless to say, he is wearing a VOTE LABOUR sticker.

The 'ow ow ow' policy is now in overdrive. HAGUE STOKES FEARS OF LABOUR LANDSLIDE, says the headline. Central Office has clearly decided that it is too late to haul up the nose of the airliner. We're flying at 25,000 feet, and falling, and we have Everest ahead. Our eyes are popping with the effort of pulling on the joystick, and the sweat is pinging off us. But we all know the truth. We're in for a prang.

So we're supplicating the electorate, to switch metaphors. Come on, we're saying. Don't do it to us. You want us to survive, don't you? You want an opposition? Then don't murder us on Thursday. The trouble with this policy is that it may well appeal to the general British sense of fair play. But what if in more sadistic breasts it also arouses a kind of Zulu killing frenzy? Maybe we are just exciting those who would never vote Tory anyway, so that otherwise apathetic Labour voters turn out just to wash their spears in the blood of Tory candidates?

* * *

Hezza speaks at the town hall, in what amounts to my eve-of-poll meeting. What a trouper. He plays a blinder, standing ramrod straight, thumbs on seam of trousers as if listening to the national anthem, and declaims, from memory, a powerful attack on Blair.

Blair just wants to be popular, Hezza says. That is his vice. That is why Labour has not made any of the difficult reforms it promised before the last election. How very different from the great Tory governments of which he was a member, says Hezza. They did not mind unpopularity. Sometimes it was the price you paid for doing the right thing.

When he has finished, he gets a pretty big hand, and Maggie Pullen turns to me with a challenging sort of beam. 'Top that,' she says.

Of course I can't top that, but I am indebted to Frank Johnson for this account, which appeared a couple of days later in the *Telegraph*: BORIS CONJURES UP TOMMY COOPER SHOW, JUST LIKE THAT, said the headline.

> I followed William Hague to Oxford West and Abingdon yesterday. The previous night I was in nearby Henley-on-Thames town hall; filled by 400 local people, huge for this campaign. Michael (now Lord) Heseltine, the outgoing MP,

> shared a platform with the (we must assume) incoming MP, Boris Johnson.
>
> It must have been a nerve-racking experience to have to share a platform with a charismatic orator both famous and notorious. Nonetheless, Lord Heseltine performed rather well. He lacked Mr Johnson's gravitas. He did not seem to know much about Tory policy. At 68, he still has much to learn.
>
> Lord Heseltine's speech was somewhat party political; about how disappointing Mr Blair had proved. As he talked on, a woman muttered: 'We've come to hear Boris, not him.' Mr Johnson's was the speech of a statesman. He dealt with the campaign's issues in a way the audience understood. He ignored them. He also made them laugh. Except, that is, Lord Heseltine. Lord Heseltine had hoped to be succeeded by someone who shared his views on Europe, but of course his local association, like Conservative associations everywhere, did not share his views on Europe, nor his views on Lady Thatcher, whom all Conservative associations worship.

And so on. I want to stress that Frank Johnson is no immediate relation of mine.

Tuesday 5 June

I've got to stop worrying, says Chris. I keep going into the office, and disturbing Pamela by riffling through the canvass returns, and having little cardiac infarcts every time I find someone who is switching from C to A.

But we have a terrific meeting in Goring, also attended by Richard Benyon, the candidate for the adjacent seat of Newbury. He's there in search of voters from Streatley, which is just over the river.

The only trouble is that owing to some mix-up, the hall has been booked by a dog-training session, and we have to cram into a small side-room. There are at least 160 people, and they are poking their heads through the windows, and queuing at the door.

John Farrow, the county council candidate, is there, and he also speaks well. There is a Lib Dem with a beard, who raises some difficult points about health.

'You keep talking about toast,' he says with mounting impatience, 'but what are you actually going to *do*?'

I try to answer him, in some detail, but nothing seems to satisfy him. 'Huh,' he groans. Luckily he is just demanding, for the third time, what I am actually going to *do*, when there is an intervention from next door.

Woof woof woof go the dogs, as though telling him to shut up and sit down. Which, amid general laughter and applause, he does. As Bill Deedes says, get the dogs on your side, and you are halfway there.

Wednesday 6 June

Finally, on the eve of poll, I meet a voter who says openly and unashamedly, without any prompting, that he thinks taxes are too high, and he is hoping the Tories will cut them.

He is a young Asian, living on an estate in Thame, and he cannot believe the burdens on his IT business. That is the view of many voters, of course, and they are right. But what has been so fascinating and depressing about this election, is the way the terms of political discourse have changed. Even Tories no longer demand tax cuts with the old full-throated conviction.

Slowly, and barely perceptibly, the phrase 'tax cut' has become a little ambiguous, and certainly no longer guaranteed to raise a cheer. It is extraordinary. This is the same electorate that mutinied over the cost of petrol, and was prepared to bring the country to its knees because of Gordon Brown's absurd fuel duty escalator. They know that taxes have gone up from 35 to almost 38 per cent of GDP. They know that Gordon Brown has raided the pension funds, and immensely complicated the entire taxation system, and still they fail to complain, and tax fails to resonate as an electoral issue. Why?

The first reason, I suppose, is that people feel rich, and that they can 'afford a bit more for good public services'. The second reason is that Labour tactics have been ingenious. They grossly overtaxed the public during the parliament, and yet they also hugely underspent.

By the time of the election, the public services were screaming for more money, and the Tory posters were quite right. 'You paid the tax – where are the nurses?' we asked. The trouble was that the elector might agree that this was a reasonable question. But he also thought that you certainly weren't going to get any more nurses by cutting tax. Which is what, on a small scale, and admittedly in areas other than health, the Tories were proposing to do.

In other words, Labour had established a brilliant political trap. The worse the public services were, the more they kept people on trolleys, the better that was for Blair, because it appeared that higher taxation was inevitable and necessary. It was a good stunt. Well done, Blair and Brown. All I can say is that they won't be allowed to pull it twice. They have taken the money. They've got to show they can use it to improve public services.

Somehow we've got to convince men like the marketing manager of Walker's Crisps that we are more than just a capitalist party that will help him sell as much deep-fried potato as he likes. He already knows that we are suspicious of Brussels, and that we will die in the last ditch to preserve the prawn cocktail flavour crisp. He already knows that we don't like too much regulation, and will try to preserve his emulsifiers and anti-oxidants.

What he wants to feel is that we are also a solid, one-nation party, who will use the tax from his vast profits to the benefit of all. He doesn't mind this stuff about bringing new money into the NHS. But he uses the NHS. He wants it to survive. He doesn't desperately want to have whacking health insurance premiums, though he might be open to persuasion that the system is in need of reform. He cannot be taken for granted. But if the Tories are to regain office, they will have to regain the trust of people like him.

Election Day

Thursday 7 June

The phone rings. I'm hunched in the kitchen at Swyncombe, eating my last breakfast as a Tory candidate. All we have left is some cheese from Asda in Wheatley. No disrespect to Archie Norman, Asda supremo and Tory bigwig, but after a couple of weeks in the fridge, it's a pretty miserable object, as cracked as a dry riverbed.

As I gnaw away, it hits me that the polls have been open for almost half an hour. Across Britain the early risers have been making their marks on the ballot paper. In South Oxfordshire the commuters are doing the business: all those people I beamed at and wooed, all deciding, marking, folding, posting and leaving the polling station with that odd quinquennial sense of having just participated, in a tiny way, in the country's future. In just fourteen and a half hours it will all be over. If I'm done for, there's not a lot I can do now to rescue the position. And to look on the bright side, there's not a lot more I can do to cock it up.

It's Soames on the phone. He wants to know how it looks. I dunno, I say. For God's sake, he says, don't tell me you think you are going to lose. Well, I don't really, not rationally, but you never know. I ask him what he plans for polling day. 'I am going to have an enormous lunch, drink two bottles of Meursault and go to sleep in my back garden,' he says. That sounds to me like a good scheme, but not one that I can imitate.

In an act of characteristic saintliness, Richard Pullen drives me round the polling stations. Marina goes with Chris in the bulbous blue Fiat loaned by GQ magazine, taking the same circuit but in the opposite direction. Our mission today is a simple one: to look in on all the committee rooms, and to thank the tellers. You don't know about tellers? You've never heard of the committee rooms? You do not know the riches of British democracy. Here's what they are doing.

The tellers, normally one from each party, sit outside the polling station, sometimes at a desk, and ask those who come and go the number of their polling cards. After about an hour of this they are relieved, and they wander back to the committee room. The committee room is a venerable institution of the Tory party, usually someone's front room, its location marked out with a big VOTE CONSERVATIVE sign, or perhaps some blue balloons. Every polling district has its own committee room, which means there are quite a few in South Oxfordshire on 7 June 2001. By tradition all those using the committee room are fortified with tea, coffee, cake and, once the sun is over the yardarm, whatever alcohol the committee room may choose. It is a scene of great confabulation, conjecture and dispute.

Into the committee room comes the teller, hotfoot from the polling station, bearing his list of numbers. These numbers are checked against the list of voters. Now, with any luck the area will have been efficiently canvassed, and the committee room will be able to establish two things: the identity of these voters on the teller's list, and whether or not they are Conservatives. Frankly, at this stage in the game, there is only one objective: to work out which known Conservatives haven't voted, and to encourage them to go to the polls. From round about five o'clock it is customary to remind people of their democratic duty – provided, of course, they are down on the canvass returns as Tory voters. You do not say, Oi, why haven't you voted yet? You say, Can we offer you a lift to the polls? To which the person may snap, 'I may be eighty-five but I can jolly well walk to the polling station, since it is just at the end of my front drive, thank you very much.'

This year, as far as I can see, there is much modernisation under way. Under Chris's Napoleonic plans the committee rooms have computers in them, and there is some suggestion that they should be renamed 'campaign centres', to give a more pro-active and forward-looking feel to the operation. Some veterans insist on using the old paper-and-pen methods. 'We'll all have died off by next time,' they tell the agent when he tries to scold them.

From the beginning, I try to work out how it is going.

'Oh, we'll be all right here,' they say. 'It's nationally that I'm worried about.'

Yes, I say, craning to look at the mass of papers, but when you say it will be all right here ...?

Well, they say, it looks as though between 40 and 50 per cent of the people voting are known Conservatives.

Really, I say. Gosh! I say, and begin to feel rather good about things.

Hang on a moment, says someone. Let's refine that. What we are saying is that, of the group of people (a) who have voted and (b) whose preferences are known, between 40 and 50 per cent have previously told us they would vote Tory.

You mean, I say, there are lots of other people voting, about whose intentions we know nothing?

Oh yes, they say.

But how many?

Oh, most people, they beam.

And a further awful thought strikes me. These people we think are going to vote Tory, according to our canvass returns – we might be wrong about them, mightn't we? They might be diddling us.

That's right, they grin, and I reflexively eat a great wad of banana bread.

At every polling station – normally a school or a community centre – it is the same ambiguous message. Electoral law thankfully forbids us from canvassing in these places. But you can sense the struggle in the expressions of the voters. Some of them shake my hand, and say good luck, or give a furtive thumbs up. But others – more than half , I'd say – keep silent and avert their eyes. And as the day goes on, it seems to be roughly the same story in every committee room. We think the Tory vote is turning out. We hope it is. But we won't really know until the early hours of tomorrow.

Every time we pass a Lib Dem roadside sign – an ugly fluorescent orange lozenge – I feel a little palpitation. I can't understand how they are permitted by English Heritage, or English Nature, or the Countryside Commission, or whoever is responsible for our hedgerows. If we Tories were less principled, less decent, less conservative, we'd do what they do to us. We'd steal out in the middle of the night and uproot the stakes, and throw them on the bonfire. And whenever we pass some VOTE CONSERVATIVE signs – a tasteful, rurally sensitive combination of rapeseed yellow and deep sky blue – I feel the anxiety subsiding. During the first few weeks you may feel embarrassed by the sight of your name desecrating the views of South Oxfordshire. As the election draws nearer, and your paranoia intensifies, it becomes a source of profound consolation.

All in all, there is something overwhelming in the sight of so many people working, for no financial reward, to the same end. Of course, they are working not so much to get me elected, as to get the county council back; but it is pretty humbling all the same. Whatever people say about the Conservative Party, it is an extraordinary organisation. It has governed Britain for the better part of the democratic epoch, and it has not, on the whole, done a bad job. We will be back.

(Pause while author sniffs, wipes nose, etc., recovers.)

But not this year. I have had the odd moment during the last four years, when I have thought it possible that we would win the next election. They only lasted about thirty seconds each. As little as a year ago it seemed inevitable that we would make a big dent in Blair's majority. Six months ago my prediction was a Labour majority of eighty. Now, though, there's something so implacable about these polls – and they are not really wrong, the polls; it's just the politicians who pretend they are wrong – that I am beginning to think something very nasty might be afoot. Sometimes I worry that the British electorate has acquired a bad habit, like the man-eaters of Tsavo. They picked up the taste for devouring innocent Tories four years ago, and maybe the hunger is on them again.

One thing that may help us, we constantly say, is the turn-out. Our troops will turn out, we tell ourselves, since they recognise the essential emptiness of Blair and New Labour; and their troops may stay at home in protest at the vanilla nothingness of Blairism. By lunchtime it is obvious that the early spurt has dried to a trickle, and the turn-out is, indeed, well down on last time.

I vote in Watlington, once for me and once for Roger Belson. It's rather tricky, the physical business of voting. You hardly dare make a mark for fear of putting it in the wrong space, and then you stare at it afterwards, sure that there must be a mistake. You also feel slightly odd voting for yourself, as if you are cheating.

By now I am just clock-watching, longing for it to be over. Three o'clock – seven more hours to go. Four o'clock – six more hours. At about six Marina and I meet up and we go for some zonk at Swyncombe. At about eight thirty we drive through the dusk to the Shepherd's Hut in Ewelme, and kill more time having supper.

And then we roll up at the Icknield School, where the count is taking place, and that's it. It's ten. *Dong*. Rien ne va plus. The electorate has spoken.

For months people have been telling me that it is a physical impossibility for me to lose Henley. Water would sooner flow uphill, leaves stay on trees, Network SouthEast trains arrive on time, the English football team defeat the Germans five–one in a World Cup qualifier – hang on, scratch that last bit. William Hague made a joke about it in a speech. 'If Boris loses Henley, then we really are in trouble!' he said, and everyone laughed uproariously at the idea.

Logically, though, it can't be excluded. In my mind's eye I constantly see the heroism of Michael Portillo, his quiff unbowed, not a tremble in those famous lips, at that dreadful moment of rejection in 1997. What will I do? Will I take it on the chin? Or will I flee blubbing to New South Wales, to take up a career selling Nature's Raw Guarana to the housewives of Wollongong?

We need no pass to get in to the count. The police,

who seem to be from Aylesbury, grin and say, 'Good evening, Mr Johnson.' They know we are for it, one way or another.

As soon as you see the ballot boxes arriving, locked and sealed, you feel the solemnity of the business. The desks are arranged in a square, filling the hall, and the counters are sitting behind the desks, dozens of them flexing their fingers and limbering up. Who are they? How are they chosen? Some of them seem to be winking. Is that because they are friendly, or teasing, or is it a bit of a tic?

We are only allowed eight supporters into the count, but Oliver Tickell says the Greens won't need to use their full ration, and we can admit some of our folk on his ticket. If this election were being conducted by single transferable vote, Oliver would definitely get my second preference.

The rule seems to be that you can walk up and down in front of the counters' desks, arms folded behind your back and looking beady. In fact, the yellow-rosetted Lib Dems are already hard at it, eyeing the papers as they fall from the boxes, like wasps on a windfall of greengages. But you can't go all the way down to the back, where the counted votes will eventually be piled. By mistake I wander into the wrong area, and am evicted by one of the assistant returning officers.

There is some sort of food, but we can't face it. The TV is babbling away, but you know how it is for the first few hours of election night: there's nothing to watch – only the pundits churning the ether with their lip-smacking anticipatory metaphors of Tory slaughter, rout, carnage, shambles, abattoir, etc. But no actual data.

So Marina and I give up on the TV, and wander back into the hall. We say hi to Janet Matthews, the Labour candidate.

We chew the fat with Oliver the Green; we pow-wow with the lads from UKIP, who are looking very chipper in their purple and yellow regalia. And we hobnob with the media. There is Tom Boyle of the *Henley Standard*, and quite a few others, including some BBC bigfoots. There is Justin Webb and, floating among us like an epiphany, a goddess: in what must rank as the highest compliment that I could be paid by the corporation which once sacked me for speaking with the wrong voice, we have Anna Ford. She is looking indescribably lovely. I have been a fan of Anna Ford ever since, as a teenager, I read *Private Eye*'s account of Reginald Bosanquet's thwarted passion for her in the ITN newsroom, called 'After the Break'. I took this account to be more or less true. Now she walks up and down carrying a large notebook … and wait!

A man with a mike comes up to me. Anna wants us. We are going to be on *Election Special.* In just a few minutes Dimbleby will be going live to Watlington. So we scramble on to the BBC's little broadcasting stage at the back, and Anna and I gaze at each other while she listens to her earpiece, waiting for the signal from London that the eyes of Britain are upon us.

This goes on for some time. I have plenty of time to observe her great beauty. She seems to have an awful lot written in her book. What is she going to ask?

After about ten minutes of solid gazing and waiting, by which time I am quite faint with admiration, a flicker of irritation crosses that lovely, heart-shaped face.

It seems there has been a change of plan in London. Something more exciting has happened in Scotland or somewhere, and we both get all un-miked up and drift off again. The results are starting to come in on the TV, all the safe Labour seats flashing up as 'Labour hold'.

In fact, this goes on for some time. It must be after midnight now, and the Tories don't seem to have won any seats at all.

Here in Watlington the interminable process of winnowing and sorting continues. We can see the ballot papers now, and quite a few seem to have been crossed in the box next to my name. Maybe it will be all right, eh? But, uh-oh, here is Catherine Bearder, the Lib Dem, wearing a bright gingham jacket. 'Well, Boris,' she says knowingly, 'it doesn't look as though you have done as well in Henley town as you thought you would.' What? How does she know? How can she tell, for heaven's sake, just by staring at these mounds of paper? Is she psychic?

It pops into my head at this point that the BBC did a dress rehearsal for this event. According to my sister-in-law Shirin Wheeler, who was there, one of the scenarios was that Boris Johnson should lose.

I go to the TV in search of consolation. In vain. We seem to have won a couple of seats, but Labour has won hundreds. In so far as there is a swing to the Tories, it seems tiny, and in some places there is even a swing against us.

I can't believe it: we seem to have lost Guildford. There is some kind of nonsense about Ann Widdecombe being in trouble in Maidstone.

Hello, it's the Beeb again. Anna wants me. We have another session of looking at each other while Dimbleby resolutely fails to come to us. I am starting to think this is a specially elaborate torture.

I don't know what time it is now. One a.m. turns into two a.m. and then it's three, and the rout goes on; or rather, an almost exact repetition of the rout last time. We have some good news. We win Taunton. I give a cheer and am ashamed to say I start taunting the Lib Dems. Well done, Adrian Flook.

My mate Benyon almost retakes Newbury. We win a seat in Scotland. Yippee.

A tap on the shoulder from Anna's man. They crank up the camera, turn on the lights, and we gaze at each other again. 'They say they may come to us in just a few minutes,' she says. But no, more bad news down the ear-piece. It looks as though Dimbleby and Marr and Professor Tony King are so amused by each other's company that they see no need to go to Watlington.

So I un-mike again, and go into a kind of trance in front of the TV. I yawn prodigiously out of nerves, with no hand in front, a real exhibition of the epiglottis. The PA snapper catches this. Oi, I say, you can't use that. The *Guardian* later uses it three times.

And then Chris seeks me out, and says that in fifteen minutes there will be a declaration. Right, I say, and try to find somewhere secluded to think of something to say when we get on the stage. About two minutes later there is a commotion. Marina wants me. The declaration is expected any minute, and I have got to get my ass down to the front of the hall, where all the other candidates have already assembled. She is not coming on stage, she says, because it has been determined that it will not bear the weight of the spouses.

Almost as soon as I get there, the deputy returning officer, Steve Lake, is reading the result.

The truth is that I already know it, roughly. I've looked at my bundles of ballot papers, each of which contain 500 votes, and I've counted them. I've counted the other two biggish piles. The Tory majority is about 8500 votes.

'I hereby declare Boris Johnson is duly elected Member of Parliament for Henley-on-Thames,' says Steve Lake.

I shake hands with all the other candidates and say:

'I want to thank the police for all their work in overseeing the process, and all you counters who have struggled on into the small hours (consult watch) – it's nearly breakfast-time now.

'It wasn't I who achieved this result, of course. It was the many people who worked on behalf of the Conservative Party, some of whom are here tonight.

'My thanks to you all, and to the people who voted for me, and to those who didn't vote for me in huge numbers. I am grateful to you all.

'This isn't the time for some kind of political analysis about the state of the Conservative Party. Suffice it to say that it has not been a brilliant night for us, but I am not going to go on about that now, because there will be other brilliant nights.

'It's lightening over there through the windows, and it is the darkest hour that comes before dawn. Bethink ye of that, all those who voted against the Tory party.

'We will be back, and we will regenerate ourselves, and I hope to play a part in that regeneration, but mainly I hope to be a good constituency MP to you all. Many thanks for the honour you have done me.

'Good morning.

'Let's go back home and prepare for breakfast.'

I suppose I should be disappointed that my majority is not as big as Hezza's. But I'm not. I'm just thrilled to have got more than 20,000 votes, and to have been comfortably in first place.

Anyway, Chris soon produces the consoling statistic that every candidate can always find in an election result. 'You've done bloody well,' he says, tapping away on his calculator. It seems that I have 46 per cent of the vote, the same as Hezza had in 1997; and the diminished majority is almost entirely attributable to a 13 per cent fall in turn-out. There is a very small 1 per cent swing to the Lib Dems, but you can tell, by looking at them, how disappointed they are not to have run me closer. They still look like wasps, but droopier, as though they have fallen into a swimming pool.

Soon I seem to be kissing or shaking hands with almost everyone. I won't hide it from you. I feel utterly terrific. But I have forgotten about Anna Ford.

Perhaps it is because she has been spurned by Dimbleby all night; perhaps because she is fed up with hanging around in this school, being forced to bat her gorgeous eyelashes at me. But she bowls me, in my view, some pretty mean balls.

'How can you expect to look after this constituency,' she concludes, 'when you can't even look after yourself?'

Journalists, eh? Can't live with them, can't live without them.

And still the night is not over. We drive through the dawn down to the Shepherd's Hut, and I'll never forget the sight of everyone – Orpwood, Felix, Chris Quinton and others – waving as we arrive. Someone shouts 'Boris Johnson – MP!' Someone else – it may have been Trollope – once said that a man could have no higher honour than to have those letters after his name. He was right.

But the best news of all comes the following day. The Tories have done very well indeed in the county council elections. John Farrow, Roger Belson, Roy Tudor-Hughes, Tony Crabbe, David Wilmshurst, Diana

Ludlow, Carol Viney, George Sanders and Brian Law all won their seats.

Chris Scott's masterplan has paid off. It was worth it, all that knocking on doors.

Westminster

It's a few days later, and we're at Westminster, for the first few days of term. I have read complaints about the Commons, that it is too much like that other ancient British institution, the public school. And there is a faintly Malory Towers mood to the conversations. 'Hallo Darrell, Hallo Alicia, Well done, Betty, I hear you gave the Liberals a good thrashing. Did you hear the bad news about Mabel? I wonder who is going to be house captain?' and so on. We are shown the ropes by the prefects, taken to our rooms, and try to remember the rules about when we may use the portcullis-headed notepaper.

But now I am sitting on the green benches, with a few of my peers, and am filled at once with the solemnity of it all. I am the first member of a thousand generations of Johnsons (or Johnsonoglus, or whatever our Turkish name was) to sit in this House. In a few minutes we will be sworn in. Over there are the men in wigs, and there are the despatch boxes, the Ark of the Covenant of British democracy. All we need is for the Speaker to arrive, and we will proceed to the government despatch box, where a woman with a wig will hand us a slightly tatty Bible.

Then we will promise to serve Her Majesty the Queen, her heirs and successors, so help me God. I do feel moved. There is a huge political job to do. We may be only the rump of the Tory party, and, in common with other rumps, we may be divided into a left portion and a right portion. But the taxpayer expects us to be vigilant, and to protect him or her from the excesses of government.

Even more importantly, there is the job of representation. I have been given the chance to speak on behalf of the people of South Oxfordshire, without fear or favour, on everything from pollution in the Ogoni delta of Nigeria to the cost of a bus ticket from Chalgrove to Wheatley. All around me are the symbols of that democracy. There are the Hansard scribes, already in place, to record anything that is said, and if necessary to buff up our grammar.

There is Mr Speaker's Chair, still empty (it's well after 9.30 now – where is the great man?), a symbol of our right to say what we want, provided we do not accuse another member directly of lying, or use unparliamentary language. There is the Mace, the very club that Hezza swung, a symbol of the Crown in Parliament, the ultimate source of authority, and the name in which everything is done. We know, in our subtle British way, that it is better to owe our loyalty to some beautiful abstraction than to the person of this or that Prime Minister or President.

You may think this sentimental, but I am overwhelmed by a feeling of pride. This may be an imperfect institution. But it stands for things I believe in, banal things like freedom of speech and association and liberal democracy; things we take for granted, but which – at the time of writing – are under attack from an enemy whose values seem very different.

These thoughts, or most of them, are passing through my head, as we sit waiting to take the Oath, when there is a terrible noise. It is a tune, music.

It is the accursed song of Vodafone and it is coming from my pocket. About ten men in tights later explain how I have violated parliamentary etiquette. Luckily the Speaker is not yet here.

ONE YEAR ON

An MP's Life

Who Flung Bun?

You know Goodfellas, the gangster film by Martin Scorsese? In my view it is one of the finest Martin Scorsese gangster films of recent years. And the finest moment in that film is when Tommy, the diminutive psychopath played by Joe Pesci, is told that he is going to be a 'Made Man'. He is going to be inducted into the elite of the Mafia world. He is going to be a kind of boss, a don, a man of respect.

We follow Tommy as he arrives at the ghastly suburban villa where the ceremony will take place. We see him smirking and shooting his new cuffs, and smoothing his new jacket collar. We witness the pride on his face as he is welcomed by the two elderly dons, also impeccably turned out, and ushered into the appointed room.

We see Tommy's eyes widen as he walks through the door. We see him look around the room, no doubt expecting to see a convocation of ancient Sicilians; and instead he sees nothing. Just an empty chamber, with a few jumbled bar stools.

In that instant, Tommy knows he is a dead man. In the last, long second and a half of his life, Tommy knows that he is to pay a price for his own violence. And we see the terrible truth dawn on his face just as *pow*? one of the old Italian codgers steps up and puts a bullet through the back of his head.

Tommy knows the bullet is coming, even though he doesn't have time to turn his neck. In that moment his whole career flashes before him, with its symmetry of bloodshed and retribution.

And you know what? I know how poor old Tommy feels. Because here I am at the Mayor's Civic Banquet in Henley one year on from the occasion described earlier in these pages. Once again it is a scene of the utmost taste and fashion, the men in black tie, the women in cocktail dresses, and the councillors and ealdormen and mayors and mayoresses of neighbouring towns all necklaced with their chains of office.

Just like last year, the proceedings are conducted by Tony Lane, still looking like a black-locked Roman emperor. Once again, I am speaking, and getting a fairly good reception. Every part of the ceremony, in short, is going like clockwork until I see, from the corner of my eye, something terrible and unexpected hurtling towards me.

It is a bread roll. Like Tommy, I know that it is now less than a second until I get whacked.

Like Tommy, I don't have time to panic. Like the deluded Mafia thug, I just have a dim sense of injustice, of a ritual perverted and turned upside down.

Like the crazed killer, I brace myself for the final impact.

But unlike Tommy, I have not the foggiest idea why anyone should want to launch a projectile at my head.

I mean, hang on a minute. Let's freeze the frame. Let's keep that bun, a proper, crusty, six-inch bun, in mid-air while we speculate about its purpose and meaning. Here I am, the MP for Henley. It is now almost a year since the election, and there has certainly (in my view) been no political goof deserving of this kind of punishment.

Who flung bun, and why? The bun is travelling towards my right cheek at a fast-medium pace, and has plainly been fired by someone sitting, like me, at the top table. The bun-bunger must therefore be sitting on my right, and there are only three possible suspects. They are two local authority bigwigs, a man and his wife, whose name I did not immediately catch when we were introduced. And there is Marina, my wife.

Anyone who has read the foregoing chapters may think that Marina has put up with quite a lot. In general, in the privacy of the kitchen, she may be justified in chucking things at my head. But if this is her revenge, it is hard to think a more devastating method.

It is one thing to be bombarded with flour or rotten tomatoes by a bunch of screaming students, their faces contorted with hate and a misunderstanding of supply-side economics. That is what we Tories expect. It is part of the job. But to be hit by one's wife, smack in the mazzard, while giving a speech in praise of Henley at the Mayor's Civic Banquet that is something from which it would be difficult, politically, to recover. Can she possibly have been so cruel?

And yet if Marina isn't the culprit, the two remaining possibilities seem even more outlandish: a brace of nice, quiet councillors! They are a husband and wife who would seem, to go by the snatches of conversation I have overheard, to spend much of their spare time experimenting with new methods of composting vegetables.

I can't quite see them now, in this frozen eternity, since my face is still locked upon my audience, and all I can see, out of the corner of my eye, is the bun. But my vague impression is that they are a charming couple in their fifties. What can I have said, what incendiary words have I used, to provoke this violence?

Let us keep that roll there in the air, let us keep the audience in a rictus of amazement, eyes popping, hands to mouth in suppressed gasps, while we review the subject matter of my speech, to see what might have been so offensive. I have been trying to explain why I am proud to represent Henley, and what the job involves. I have been initially talking about parliament, and my experience of it over the last year. What exactly have I said? I can't remember, but here is the sort of thing I might have said. See if you can spot something which might have offended one of the three suspects.

I think I was probably talking about life at Westminster, and I think I might have mentioned PAGERS. I am not one of those lordly types, like Soames, who refuses to carry a pager. It is true that I may have written a few columns accusing the Labour backbenchers of being a bunch of prozac-munching morons, so addicted are they to the throbbing little electronic guide in their pocket. But I have to tell you, after a year of struggling to find out what is going on, that the gizmo is very useful. It alerts you to what is coming up, and when the votes are expected, and after a while you start to feel quite naked without it. In fact, I have just realised my pager is in my jacket pocket on the other side of the room. Let me just get it. Ah.

It says, 'Adjournment. Deputy Chief Whip'. That means we can all relax. Without the pager, we Tories would not have been able to achieve, as we did the other day, an improbable victory over the government. David Curry, the Tory MP for Skipton and Ripon, has an excellent bill, to allow you more flexibility with your pension when you turn seventy-five. Under the Curry plan, you would no longer be forced to buy an annuity, which is not only poor value these days, but is also swallowed up by the insurance company when you die. How to get that one past the Treasury, when you only have 166 MPs and Labour has 440?

It required generalship. It was a Friday morning, and the Labour MPs had bunked off. A few dozen Tory troops were ready for the ambush. Every so often we received a message on our pagers, such as 'Avoid tea-room or Chamber; wait until summoned.' So we lurked, while in the Chamber a handful of people debated pensions with every appearance of torpor; and then surprise! out of our foxholes we swarmed, like Vietnamese soldiers in the Tet offensive. We won by 62 votes to 8, and received congratulatory messages on our little buzzing friends. 'Well done,' said the pagers. 'Labour furious!'

It was not a decisive victory. The government, with its huge majority, can always overturn the measure. But it made a nice change from being thrashed night after night.

No, my objection to pagers is not that they go off, but that they go off at the wrong time. Sometimes they groan and vibrate all night, robotically informing you of what you already know and refusing to be turned off so that you long to bury them at the bottom of the garden. Quite often they will tell you of a vote which has just happened. Quite often they get lost, and by the time you find them there is a three day old message saying, 'See me immediately. Chief Whip.'

Which brings us to the tricky topic of the WHIPs. 'Oooh' said my colleague Bruce Anderson, when I announced that I intended to be a fairly independent parliamentarian, 'just wait till the whips get hold of you.' Huh, I scoffed. Whips! I feared no whips, I told him. Since then, it has been made perfectly clear by the Whips, in the nicest possible arm-round-the-shoulder whisky-breathing way, that they aren't going to take any nonsense from some jumped-up hack. Whips, I have discovered, make their feelings known. They describe you in Anglo-Saxon terms. They have deep and subtle ways of making your life more complicated. There was at least one moment when I found myself being physically propelled into the opposite voting lobby to the one I had initially chosen.

But one can see, upon mature reflection, what they are trying to do. They are trying to make sure a collection of 166 disparate egomaniacs all shoot from the same trench. They are trying to keep discipline and why not? They have no real sanctions. They have nothing to appeal to except our better nature, and they don't instinctively believe that we possess any such thing.

And talking of VOTING, I really wonder whether the system is beyond improvement. If there is a disagreement about a bill, the Speaker calls for a division and everyone then spends about quarter of an hour milling around in the oak-panelled lobbies, sniffing each other like terriers. If you have four votes, it can take up to an hour. Voting can start at 10pm and finish at 11. Is it beyond the wit of man to devise some speedier method?

While I am whingeing, I might mention the discomforts of waiting to SPEAK. Everybody who wants to speak must tell the Speaker, and then sit in the debate until called. This is fine, except it is quite usual to find oneself sitting for seven and a half hours, and then not being called because some Lib dem crasher hogs the time.

You could always bunk off to the TEA-ROOM, which is terrific. It is positively scandalous how cheap our tea is. The biscuits are an outrageous bargain. Does the taxpayer know how much he is subsidising us? But you run the risk, if you spend too long in the tea-room, that the SPEAKER will move you down the list, and you won't get a chance to electrify the House with your thoughts. This punishment, by the way, is quite correct. If you believe you have something to contribute to a debate, you should damn well listen to everyone else's contributions.

When you are called to speak, you must remember to use the correct FORMS OF ADDRESS. No one is addressed in the vocative except the Speaker, and everyone else is referred to in the third person, even if they are sitting in front of you. The purpose of this, I imagine, is to maintain an air of dignity. So you must not say, 'You four-eyed git'. You must say, 'I hope the Hon Member is aware, Mr Speaker, that he is a four-eyed git.' In a recent speech on the Budget I kept forgetting this, by referring to 'Gordon Brown', instead of to 'the Chancellor', and the Speaker (in this case the Deputy Speaker) kept ruling me out of Order.

He does this by rising to his feet and bellowing Order, at which point you must sit down. You must not be on your feet at the same time as the Speaker. Incidentally, Michael Martin has been the subject of much undeserved criticism in the *Daily Mail*, mainly because of his thick Scottish accent. I won't hear a word against him, and I bet most of my colleagues would agree.

If you fail to catch his eye, and you yearn to speak in the Commons, then you may find that the whips are very kind to you, and put you on a COMMITEE. I was lucky enough to serve for thirty-six two and a half hour sessions of the Proceeds of Crime Bill. It used to begin at five to nine on a Thursday, which is a pretty ungodly hour for someone accustomed to journalism. This is a bill, broadly speaking, to allow the state to confiscate the property of criminals, even when it isn't wholly demonstrable that the assets were paid for with criminally acquired dosh.

Suffice it to say that the Tories, especially Dominic Grieve and Nick Hawkins, argued consistently for decency and humanity, while Labour accused us of being soft on criminals. The most important event was the breakdown, in January, of the central heating. Mind you, there are times, when all 659 MPs are assembled in the Chamber, that it has the clammy heat of the reptile house at London Zoo.

While we are dishing out compliments, I want to say something in praise of MEMBERS OF PARLIAMENT. You may think this self-serving from a journalist who has become a politician, but these boys and girls in Westminster get a far worse press than they deserve. There is one Tory MP with a military bearing, and an air of infinite reliability. He is exactly the man you would want on a tiger-shoot. No one, at first glance, would call him an intellectual, and yet I was chatting to him over tea, and blow me down, he is the world's number one expert on the life and works of Dostoevsky. They have hidden depths, these MPs.

There is another man, a huge Labour MP from Glasgow, a testimony to the benefits of the fried Mars Bar. He stood up in the middle of a debate on pensions, and just blew the Labour minister away with a closely argued analysis of the Advance Corporation Tax and the FRS17 accounting procedure, as well as other Labour goofs which will impoverish future generations of pensioners. He was dynamite, and talking of SPEECHES, you may be wondering how my own contributions are going.

Someone once told me to remember, whenever I stood up, to speak for Henley and South Oxfordshire. So I have. I have spoken on schools in South Oxfordshire, the closure of nursing homes in South Oxfordshire, pubs in South Oxfordshire, the Ridgeway path which runs through the place, the Henley Community Online Centre, the Culham Nuclear Research lab, Oxfordshire housing problems, bus routes, the Watlington hospital, the preservation of the Landfill Tax Credit Scheme which has done so much to help repair the lych-gates of Oxfordshire and so on.

Not all these interventions have gone well. I was

asking an important question the other day about nuclear fusion, and was completely put off my stroke by some Luddite barracking from the member for Glasgow Pollock. In case you can't place him, he is almost totally bald, giving him a curiously buttock-headed appearance.

After you have spoken, an old hand will often give you a piece of ADVICE. I love advice. 'Speak more slowly,' one chap told me. Apparently the optimum tempo is a sort of Alistair Cooke, just above stalling speed.

It is always good, too, when people give you advice 'as a friend'. I just want to tell you as a friend that your speech was hopeless. I just want to tell you as a friend that you are a prat. And so on.

These, then, are the kind of reflections on which my speech may be based, as I stand there, about to be hit by a bun. They may be trivial. But is there anything you can see which is so offensive as to provoke one of the three suspects (Marina, two councillors) to pelt me with pastry? Of course not.

So perhaps it was something to do with my remarks about Henley, and my work in the constituency. Let me see. What have I been saying?

Perhaps I have been saying something about the MAILBAG, which is huge. According to Melissa, my secretary, who is a genius, it is about three times as big as the post bag of some other MPs. Some are letters complaining about my personal appearance ('Mr Johnson, I do not wish to be rude, but...'). Sometimes you can solve the problem directly, and we have had some modest success with passport problems, citizenship problems, painting in double yellow lines, chopping down dangerous trees, quashing parking tickets, and that kind of thing. But mainly you discover that the MP is the clearing-house for the woes of the world. Your job is to forward the correspondence, with a covering letter summarising the issue, to the right person in the District Council, the County Council, or in Whitehall. It is amazing how swiftly and fully the civil servants respond. I wouldn't say it always means a result; but at least it gives you an idea of what is bugging people.

In the first few months we received a great many letters from people worried about the possible closure of the Landfill Tax Credit Scheme, of which I had not previously been aware. So we applied for a debate in Westminster Hall, and succeeded. A minister, Mr Paul Boateng, came to respond for the government. For half an hour we harangued him about the wonders of the Landfill Tax Credit Scheme.

This is a measure by which a tax on landfill can be used by local bodies to beautify the environment a kind of compensation for having London's nappies buried in giant holes in Oxfordshire. It is very popular, because it gives local people wide discretion in how to spend the money. Think of the water-meadows, we told Boateng. Think of the water-cress beds at Ewelme, the Norman church spires, the village halls which have been repointed and improved under this beneficent scheme. Think of the lych-gates and playgrounds!

Boateng rolled his eyes plaintively. The government was hoping to scrap the scheme, and use the money to encourage recycling. A few months later, if you consult the latest Budget red book, it would appear that the scheme has been reprieved. I am not saying that this was a Johnson triumph, but you can't entirely rule it out, can you?

And while we are on the subject of Oxfordshire countryside, I think I may have been talking to the Civic Banquet about the beauty of my constituency. It is looking especially lovely just now, with the candles on the chestnuts, and the blossom like rolling clouds on the Chilterns. It is possible that I have just said that people keep telling me how lucky I am to be the MP for Henley, and how much I agree with them. They can't possibly object to that, can they?

Maybe I have just been talking about surgeries, and saying how much I enjoy them. It is true that Michael

Heseltine gave a more than usually wolfish chuckle, when he passed on a couple of the dossiers to me. But we have doubled the number of surgeries, and rotate them round the constituency, and they are very productive. Don't you feel a bit like a social worker? someone asked me.

Well, if you've been a journalist, intruding on private grief and carving people up, you don't mind feeling like a social worker from time to time.

So there you are. There is the gist of what I have been saying to the audience in Henley Town Hall, still looking very pretty with its white plaster mouldings and eggshell blue paint, and still full of people watching the trajectory of the bun.

As you will accept, there has been nothing much that is controversial, and nothing to justify the attack.

It is only at the end of my speech, long after the roll finds its mark – it stings, by the way – that I find out the culprit. No, it isn't Marina. Whatever my crimes, she hasn't done it, not that night, not with the bread roll.

It is the councillor! And it is the woman! Unbelievable. Mrs Hards, she turns out to be called, and rather fittingly. She is the Labour chairperson of the district council, and appears to be a woman of wrath.

She says my speech is too political, and, OK, I suppose I have also said quite a lot of stuff about the Blair government's failure to improve public services. In retrospect, I should have done what I did the year before keep it to a simple hymn of praise to Henley.

But what the hell: I thought I was outlining some top policies, on health, education, crime, transport and other things, which will one day propel the Tories to power. The only conclusion I can offer is that Mrs Hards was just frightened by the range and fertility of the Tory agenda.

I think she saw power slipping away from the Labour government. She panicked. Confounded in argument, she resorted to an inarticulate act of political violence.

As I am able to tell the Henley Standard, her actions prove that the Tories are on a roll.

This book has been an attempt to explain why a person, in full possession of his or her senses, should want to become an MP. It may be that there are some readers so suspicious of politicians that they cannot believe anyone would want the job, except power-maniacs, freaks and whackos. I have no answer to them. I could attempt to deny falling into any of these categories, but am conscious that my denials might not be accepted.

All I can say is that there are moments when I am convinced that it is by far the best job I have ever had, and that the real eccentrics are the people who don't want to become Members of Parliament. With glacial slowness I am beginning to understand how it all works, and which levers of the constitution have pulleys attached to them, and which ones are only there for show.

It is far too early to draw any conclusions. But I have one preliminary hunch. There is far too much bilge talked about the end of representative democracy. People are constantly telling us that parliament is losing its influence, ceding authority to the media, the judiciary, the EU institutions, ludicrous regional assemblies, non-governmental organisations, Cherie Blair, and all the rest of it. I wonder.

There is certainly a struggle going on, between all these zones of influence; and it is true that parliament has not been doing especially well in recent years. But this is a long, historic struggle, in which the people's representatives have previously competed with the Crown, or the Church. There are ebbs and flows. As I look around the Green Benches at my fellow-MPs, some crapulous, some bright-eyed, some brilliant, some bonkers, I do not doubt for a second that parliament is capable of fighting back.

Acknowledgements

My thanks go above all to the officers and members of the South Oxfordshire Conservative Association. Thanks also to Leonard and Rosalind Ingrams for their hospitality; to Charles Moore and Mark Stanway for their kindness. My apologies to all those whose efforts I have failed to recognise in this partial and episodic account, and apologies to anyone I have accidentally traduced. Thanks also to Melissa Crawshay-Williams, my secretary at the Commons, and Catriona Lothian, for her researches. I owe particular and humble thanks to Conrad Black, Daniel Colson, and others involved with the *Spectator*, of whom I might single out Ann Sindall, Stuart Reid, Petronella Wyatt, Lucy Vickery, Vanessa Tyrell-Kenyon, Kimberley Fortier, Arthur, Mark, Liz, Heath, Emma, Clare, (choke, sob) my old English teacher, (blub) the man who makes my sandwiches...